Taking slightly early retirement after forty years in teaching has led Howard Peach to spend time pursuing interests not directly concerned with education. He has written books, articles, stories and poems about schools, pupils, relationships, humour, dialect, local history and events. He enjoys browsing, walking and talking and exploring the countryside. A lifetime's absorption in people, places and things has led him inexorably, perhaps, to this present collection of *Lincolnshire Curiosities,* which is the result of a year spent in touring the county, gathering information and taking the photographs in the book.

Following Page.
Heckington Mill (See No 18).

Lincolnshire Curiosities

Howard Peach

THE DOVECOTE PRESS

First published in 1994 by The Dovecote Press Ltd
Stanbridge, Wimborne, Dorset BH21 4JD

ISBN 1 874336 22 9

© Howard Peach 1994

Phototypeset in Times by The Typesetting Bureau
Wimborne, Dorset
Printed and bound by Biddles Ltd
Guildford and Kings Lynn

Contents

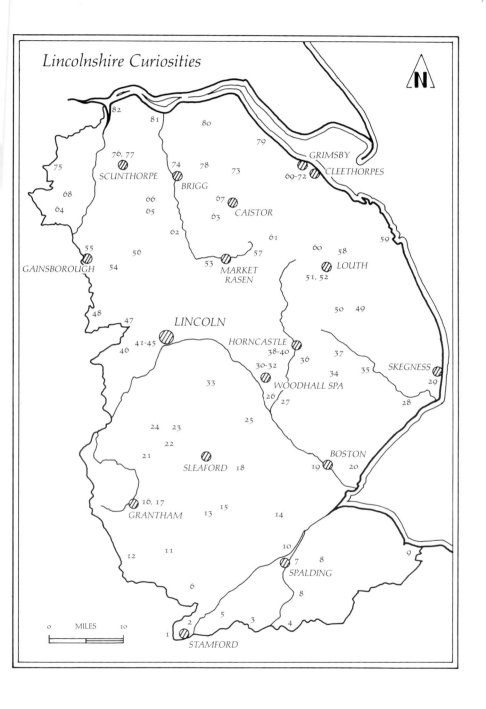

Lincolnshire Curiosities

82
81
80
79
76, 77
SCUNTHORPE
75
74
78
73
GRIMSBY
69-72
CLEETHORPES
68
BRIGG
67
64
66
65
CAISTOR
63
62
61
59
55
56
57
53
60
58
GAINSBOROUGH
54
MARKET
RASEN
51, 52
LOUTH
48
47
LINCOLN
50
49
41-45
HORNCASTLE
46
38-40
37
36
35
SKEGNESS
30-32
34
29
33
WOODHALL SPA
28
26
27
25
24
23
22
21
19
BOSTON
20
SLEAFORD
18
16, 17
15
GRANTHAM
13
14
11
10
12
7
8
9
SPALDING
6
8
2
5
3
4
1
STAMFORD

0   MILES   10

Introduction

Let me own straight away that I am not a 'Yellowbelly' born and bred. But for forty years I have lived in the neighbouring counties of Nottinghamshire, Norfolk and East Yorkshire, so there is always a freshness and a delight in making frequent visits.

Many of my childhood memories are of trips to Lincoln or Skegness. I learned early to look out for landmarks like Grantham Railway Station, Boston Stump, the Wash and, triumphantly, Skeggy's Clock Tower. During World War Two I thrilled to hear from 'Bomber County' of stirring events that began at RAF Waddington and Scampton. In later years I came to a growing appreciation of the manifold attractions of England's second largest county, with its distinctive panoramas – the Fens, mysterious, rich in haunting landscapes; the Isle of Axholme with ancient turbaries and vestiges of medieval strip farming; magnificent coastal sands and salt marshes; and the Wolds, a designated area of Outstanding Natural Beauty.

Even now I still marvel that Lincolnshire offers so much to those who love old towns. So often history and tradition reach back across the centuries. Of the five 'Danish' towns of the old Danelaw, two were in Lincolnshire – Lincoln and Stamford. As for the villages, one has but to run an eye casually across the map to note the prevalence of settlements ending with the Danish suffix '-by'. Beautiful places by the score await discovery but not, I pray, commercialisation. And there are plenty of wonderful place-names to savour, like Silk Willoughby, Claxby Pluckacre and Mavis Enderby. Local dialects are rich and good-humoured, spiced with much homespun wisdom.

Country ways, ancient traditions, unusual museums, stately homes, glorious churches .... we lack not for things that are enduring and curious. Whilst I am grateful to many people and myriad sources, the final selection has to be mine. I hope that this book will remind and inform Lincolnshire enthusiasts, whether residents or visitors, of the range and variety of 'curiosities' within the county, and prompt, perhaps, further exploration and research.

Acknowledgements

At this late stage in the preparation of a book one realises again how much is due to the generous expertise of so many people. The staffs of heritage and information centres, museums and libraries have been instructive and resourceful. I am particularly grateful to the Humberside Archaeology Unit at Beverley for information on Gainsthorpe Deserted Village and the Kirton Lime Kiln; to the museum staff at Scunthorpe for advice on Dragonby; and to Ayscoughee Hall Museum for guidance on Spalding. Lt. Col. J. L. M. Dymoke, MBE, DL of Scrivelsby Court was kind enough to provide me with valuable detail on the Office of Royal Champion of England. Of the new friends one makes in this kind of enquiry I must mention Mr. G. W. H. Hadfield, BEM of Alford who offered many insights on crime and punishment; and Father Terry Steele, Vicar of Weston who kindly photographed the 'Hudd' at Quadring.

For permission to use copyright photographs I am indebted to the following: Lincolnshire County Council Recreational Services – Stamford Museum (Daniel Lambert), Lincoln Castle (Prison Chapel), Local Studies Collection, Lincoln Central Reference Library (Lincoln Imp), Lincoln Museum of Lincolnshire Life (Alkborough Maze). The Humber Keel and Sloop Preservation Society ('Amy Howson'). Cambridge University Collection of Air Photographs (Gainsthorpe). Boston Guildhall Museum (White Loaf Hall). Dr. Douglas Gyte, (the Lighthouse on Guy's Head). The cover photograph of Tattershall Castle was kindly taken by Nigel Rutter.

I should like to acknowledge, too, Skegness Town Council for their help with the Jolly Fisherman.

Finally, my thanks are due to Mr. David Burnett of the Dovecote Press Ltd. for his patient help and advice in bringing this work to fruition.

Daniel Lambert.

1 The World's Heaviest Man

Position: Stamford
O.S. Map: Kettering and Corby, Sheet No. 141
Map Ref: TF 030/072
Access: Stamford Museum is readily found on Broad Street.

This enormous model is life-size and dressed in the original clothes of the great man. Son of the huntsman of the Earl of Stamford, Daniel Lambert was born at Blue Boar Lane in March 1770. Despite a moderate diet, he soon began putting on weight, reaching thirty-two stone by the age of twenty-three. Eventually he was obliged to give up his job as keeper at the Leicester Bridewell Prison, and the last years of his life were spent mainly at his London home, where curious visitors paid a shilling to see him. While visiting the races at Stamford in 1809 he died at the Waggon and Horses Inn, exhausted by his weight of 52 stone 11 lb, and a still expanding waistline of 112 inches. It is said that a wall and window of the inn had to be demolished before his coffin could be removed.

Daniel's grave is in St. Martin's Churchyard. His huge walking stick and portrait are displayed in the George Hotel across the High Street.

Places of Interest in the Neighbourhood
2. The Scholars' Gate (Stamford)
3. Lob's Pound (Deeping St. James)
5. Crowns, Elephants and Maidens (Greatford)

2 The Scholars' Gate

Position: Stamford
O.S. Ref: Kettering and Corby, Sheet No. 141
Map Ref: TF 034/075
Access: On St. Paul's Street the gate forms part of the wall in front of Stamford School.

For two years during the fourteenth century Stamford's Brazenose Hall became a university to rival Oxford. Oxford scholars, disgruntled by living and working conditions, migrated in 1333 to Stamford, setting up new relationships with the colleges of the Black and Grey Friars. Displeased by their secession, the Oxford authorities appealed to Edward III, who ordered the break-away students to disband and return. They did so, leaving behind an impressive brass knocker, originally brought from Brazenose College. It remained in Stamford until 1890 when it was restored to the alma mater. The present knocker was given by the Fellows of Brazenose to record the secession: note the 'brazen nose'. Until the end of the nineteenth century Oxford graduates were required to promise not to teach at Stamford.

Places of Interest in the Neighbourhood
1. The World's Heaviest Man (Stamford)
3. Lob's Pound (Deeping St. James)
5. Crowns, Elephants and Maidens (Greatford)

Brazenose Gate, Stamford.

3 Lob's Pound

Position: Deeping St. James
O.S. Map: Peterborough, Sheet No. 142
Map Ref: TF 157/096
Access: The lock-up is situated at the junction of Eastgate and Church Street.

In past times many communities found it expedient to have a small lock-up where minor offenders could cool off for a few hours. At a time when a number of gin drinkers were found drowned in ditches in the Deeping area, speedy arrest and temporary incarceration could be seen as a humanitarian gesture. The tightly-arranged bars made it impos-

The old lock-up at Deeping St. James.

sible for further refreshment to reach those in the lock-up. By peering through on the north side you can see three rounded alcoves with stone seats to which prisoners could be chained.

The Deeping St. James lock-up has survived well. In Victorian times it had housed a pump, later serving as a market cross. It is a considerable curiosity, as well as an ancient monument and a listed building.

Another intriguing lock-up is the small 'pepper pot' at Digby, opposite the church (TF 082/548).

Places of Interest in the Neighbourhood
1. The World's Heaviest Man (Stamford)
2. The Scholars' Gate (Stamford)
4. Trinity Bridge (Crowland)
5. Crowns, Elephants and Maidens (Greatford)

Trinity Bridge, Crowland.

4 Trinity Bridge

Position: Crowland
O.S. Map: Boston and Spalding, Sheet No. 131
Map Ref: TF 239/1O2
Access: Market Place crossroads.

It is thought that this remarkable architectural oddity was built by local monks between 1360 and 1390. Sir Nikolaus Pevsner, quoting Gough, has called it "the greatest curiosity in Britain, if not in Europe". Three semi-circular arches rise from a triangular base, uniting to form a single groined arch. Once boats passed beneath these arches. Centuries ago three roads met at a confluence of the River Welland and the Cat-twater Drain, continuing on to Peterborough, Stamford and Spalding. Nowadays the stream is subterranean, leaving the bridge high and dry.

The Bridge was once surmounted by a large cross and the crowned effigy on the south wall has been variously identified as (a) Our Lord holding the world in His hand) (b) the Virgin Mary and Child) (c) King Ethelbald holding a loaf. It seems to have been brought here during the eighteenth century from the west front of Crowland Abbey.

Places of Interest in the Neighbourhood
3. Lob's Pound (Deeping St. James)
5. Crowns, Elephants and Maidens (Greatford)

5 Crowns, Elephants and Maidens

Position: Greatford lies some five miles north-east of Stamford.
O.S. Map: Grantham, Sheet No. 13O
Map Ref: TF 085/118
Access: Main Street of the village.

This attractive village displays a strikingly original collection of un-usual stone carvings and artefacts, beginning to the west with pairs of decorative mushrooms. Outside the Hare and Hounds Inn is a remark-able stone sofa. By the beck, in a garden just opposite, a cross guards a small bridge. A few yards further along, each of the two old cot-tages has a large crown, florally embellished, in the front garden, com-memorating the coronation of King George VI in 1936. Next door the gate portals are stone crowned. Back over the road again the garden's centre-piece is a large stone coronet.

On and on it goes.... local folk will refer you to elephants, obelisks, wall reliefs, maidens. The approach road to the church displays several tubs and miscellaneous stonework resembling masonry that has some-how fallen intact. One square bowl to the right is ornamented by two naked maids. Two more bowls by the churchyard gates show captivat-ing spiral twists on the corners.

Adjacent, left, is the Hall where these lively Disneyesque creations were designed in the 1930's by Major C.C.L. FitzWilliams, an amateur landscape artist who also used the Chelsea Flower Show to advertise his talents. He tried his hand, too, at roof gardens, and it was he who started the village's watercress industry. He bequeathed to posterity a village rich in sculptured curiosities.

Places of Interest in the Neighbourhood
1. The World's Heaviest Man (Stamford)
2. The Scholars' Gate (Stamford)
3. Lob's Pound (Deeping St. James)

A Garden Crown, Greatford.

6 Sheltered Stocks

Position: Witham on the Hill, five miles south-west of Bourne
O.S. Map: Grantham, Sheet no. 130
Map Ref: TF 054/166
Access: On the edge of the village Green, opposite St. Andrew's
Church.

Under an Act of 1405 every town and village was required to mount
a set of stocks. Such offenders as drunks, cheating stallholders, blas-
phemers and Sunday gamesters were thus secured for a few hours open
to scorn, ridicule and sometimes unpleasant missiles. Certainly justice
was seen to be done.

The Witham stocks, of uncertain age, could accommodate two per-
sons. The shelter's skilful woodwork and immaculate tiling show a high
degree of craftsmanship. This is a beautifully landscaped corner against
the backdrop of a large village green and a thirteenth-century church.

Counsel on good behaviour is displayed across the 1847 School (now
village hall), next to the church: "TRAIN UP A CHILD THE WAY
HE SHOULD GO. WHEN HE IS OLD HE WILL NOT DEPART
FROM IT".

Other interesting stocks are to be found in St. Andrew's Church,
Folkingham (TF 071/337); and St Peter's Church, Threekingham (TF
089/362). Two restored examples are at Alvingham, at the junction of
Highbridge Road and Church Lane (TF 364/913); and in the market
place at Alford (TF 455/759).

Places of Interest in the Neighbourhood
5. Crowns, Elephants and Maidens (Greatford)
11. An Auctioneer's Epitaph (Corby Glen)

Picturesque stocks at Witham on the Hill.

7 The Dutch Connection

Position: Spalding
O.S. Map: Boston and Spalding, Sheet No. 131
Map Ref: TF 262/228
Access: The High Bridge over the River Welland is on the eastern side of the town.

This riverside area, with its seven bridges, will remind many visitors of Amsterdam. The attractive footbridge alongside the 1838 High Bridge is beautifully decorated with rows of hanging baskets and is a worthy civic showpiece. The nearby red-brick terraces, especially the small hotels in Welland Place and the Georgian dwellings of Welland Terrace, do much to enhance the Continental flavour.

Prior to local government re-organisation in 1974, Spalding was in the administrative Part of Holland (the other Lincolnshire Parts being Kesteven and Lindsey). It is very much a region of fields and dykes. The Dutch connection may be traced back to the seventeenth century when the Dukes of Bedford invited distinguished engineers like Cornelius Vermuyden to supervise the drainage of the Fens. Another of the so-called 'Adventurers' was Sir Philibert Vernatti, whose Drain on the north side of Spalding runs from the mouth of the Welland to Pode Hole.

During the depression of the 1930's a number of Dutchmen who came to Lincolnshire's Holland in search of work brought a new expertise to an established bulb industry. Since 1959 early May has heralded Tulip Time and the fabulous Flower Parade for whose floats some ten million tulip heads are used. The design of the parades was undertaken by members of the Van Driel family, artist-designers from Amstelveen, Holland; and this inspirational link has been continued by a younger generation.

Places of Interest in the Neighbourhood
8. Two Boundary Stones (Moulton, Cowbit)
10. The Pinchbeck Engine (Pinchbeck)

8 Two Boundary Stones

1. THE ELLOE STONE

Position: One mile north-east of Moulton
O.S. Map: Boston and Spalding, Sheet No. 131
Map Ref: TF 313/247
Access: Down Spalding Gate, off the north side of the A151. The stone is situated at the edge of a field.

The inscription reads: "Erected in Anglo-Saxon times to indicate the Meeting of the Hundred of Elloe Courts. Presented to the Moulton Parish Council by F. Dring Esq. (Landowner) and mounted here by public subscription on June 22nd, 1911, the day of the Coronation of George V".

It is believed that the Wapentake of Elloe was the largest in the county. Whether folk meetings were held on this site is uncertain. Life had to be adjusted to changing circumstances e.g. floodwaters. Part of this area was flooded by high tides, drowning hundreds of sheep in December, 1765.

The Elloe Stone near Moulton.

St. Guthlac's Stone at Queen's Bank, south of Cowbit.

2. ST GUTHLAC'S CROSS

Position: Queen's Bank Crossroads, 2½ miles south of Cowbit
O.S. Map: Boston and Spalding, Sheet No. 131
Map Ref: TF 260/149
Access: Via the A1073 Spalding-Crowland road. The Cross stands on a slightly elevated south-west angle of the crossroads.

Guthlac was a nobleman's son, who after serving under King Ethelred of Mercia, turned to religion, entering Repton Abbey, Derbyshire. He later founded a Benedictine hermitage amongst the swamps and solitude of Crowland, which in turn became the basis of the first Abbey, built just after his death in AD 714.

The stone, inscribed HANC PETRA GUTHLAC, is thought to be one of a number of boundary crosses set up to mark the Abbey's sphere of influence in medieval times. An occasional assertion of territorial rights by the abbot was felt to be necessary, as disputes with other foundations like Peterborough Abbey and Spalding Priory were not unknown.

A sculptured quatrefoil over the west door of the ruined nave of Crowland Abbey illustrates the life of St. Guthlac.

Places of Interest in the Neighbourhood
7. The Dutch Connection (Spalding)
10. The Pinchbeck Engine (Pinchbeck)

9 A Treasure Hunter's Dive?

Position: Guy's Head, two miles north of Sutton Bridge
O.S. Map: Boston and Spalding, Sheet No. 131
Map Ref: TF 492/257
Access: Cross Sutton Bridge and bear immediately left, following the right embankment of the River Nene north to the Wash.

The Head derives its name from Guy's Hospital, London which used to own the land. Cargo ships from Germany and Scandinavia are sometimes to be found moored at Port Sutton Bridge. Just below the junction with the Wash are two 'lighthouses', known locally as 'the follies', one on either bank. They were built in 1826 to commemorate the work of Tycho Wing in excavating this new channel for the River Nene.

During the 1930's this easterly lighthouse was occupied by Sir Peter

The Eastern Lighthouse, Guy's Head.

Scott, the naturalist and painter who made his first bird sanctuary here. The Peter Scott Walk, opened in 1989, extends for ten miles from the east bank lighthouse around the marshy shores of the Wash to the ferry at West Lynn. The area's abundant wild life includes waders, knott, dunlin, oyster catchers, Brent and pink-footed geese and the largest group of seals in Europe.

On 12 th October, 1216 while crossing the old River Nene, King John lost his baggage, the crown jewels and almost his life. His reprieve was brief as he died at Newark on 19th October. Somewhere in these waters, then – or, conceivably, beneath the plough – the treasures he lost still await discovery. Meanwhile, the journey to this far corner of the County is amply repaid in terms of natural beauty and interest.

Places of Interest in the Neighbourhood
7. The Dutch Connection (Spalding)
8. Two Boundary Stones (Moulton, Cowbit)

A glimpse of the mighty Pinchbeck Engine.

10 The Pinchbeck Engine

Position: Pinchbeck, just to the north of Spalding
O.S. Map: Boston and Spalding, Sheet No. 131
Map Ref: TF 262/262
Access: From the A16 turn down Wardentree Lane for about one mile, then left onto West Marsh Road. The Engine Museum is open daily, 10.00 am – 4.00 pm, April-October.

During the nineteenth century many pumping stations were necessary to drain this Southern Fenland. Pinchbeck's was erected in 1833 and worked until 1952. The restored, steam-driven beam-engine activates a scoop wheel with a 22ft. diameter, and is the last of its type still in situ. Attached to the wheel are forty wooden ladles, each five feet long. As the power is switched on, and the great wheel slowly turns, the visitor becomes aware of the cogs, levers and revolving spheres of well-oiled precision engineering.

   Since 1988 there has also been a Land Drainage Museum here; several areas are used to display techniques of drainage and embanking. The Museum's unique collection of tools vary in size, from a piling-frame for erecting platforms in water down to four pairs of ice skates and an eel glaive. Outside is a Priestman Cub Mk.IV Dragline Excavator from 1944, when wartime conditions demanded yet more land to be drained for agriculture.

   The site is owned and maintained by the Welland and Deeping Internal Drainage Board.

Places of Interest in the Neighbourhood
7. The Dutch Connection (Spalding)
8. Two Boundary Stones (Moulton, Cowbit)

11 An Auctioneer's Epitaph

Position: Corby Glen
O.S. Map: Grantham, Sheet No. 130
Map Ref: TF 002/250
Access: The Churchyard of St. John the Evangelist is off Moreley's
Lane.

Some fifteen yards up the path from the south porch, the headstone,
second left, bears a famous epitaph:

> Beneath this stone facetious wight
> Lies all that's left of poor Joe Wright.
> Few hearts with greater kindness warmed,
> Few heads with knowledge more informed.
> With brilliant wit and humour broad
> He pleased the Peasant, Squire or Lord.
> At length old Death with visage queer
> Assumed Joe's trade of auctioneer.
> Made him the lot to practise on
> With going, going and anon
> He knocked him down. So poor
> Joe's gone.

Prior to his death in 1835 at the age of 60, the auctioneer Joe Wright
lived in Corby, enjoying enormous personal and professional esteem
across the county. He would have presided over innumerable auctions
at the annual October Sheep Fair, which had originated in a Royal
Charter of 1238. Held during the week of the anniversary of Joe's
death, the Fair continues to flourish, with sheep sales, parades and
exhibitions.

Joseph Wright must frequently have rested his legs for a while on the
steps of the ancient market cross, itself of special architectural and
historical interest. It was once the focus of a butter market, and well
into the twentieth century was the scene of the annual May hirings of
farm workers.

Places of Interest in the Neighbourhood
6. Sheltered Stocks (Witham)
12. Genius and Graffiti (Woolsthorpe by Colsterworth)

12 Genius and Graffiti

Position: Woolsthorpe by Colsterworth
O.S. Map: Grantham, Sheet No. 130
Map Ref: SK 925/245
Access: Woolsthorpe Manor is reached via Water Lane. Owned by the
National Trust, it is open Wednesday to Sunday afternoons from
Easter to October.

Woolsthorpe Manor is a place of pilgrimage,for it was the birthplace
– on Christmas Day, 1642 – of one of the world's supreme mathe-
maticians and scientists, Isaac Newton. Newton was a weak baby, so
small that, according to his widowed mother, he could easily have been
put into a quart pot. But he showed early skill as a model maker. His
water clock, carriage, windmill and sundial earned more praise than his
lighted lanterns floated perilously by a kite. After some years at Kings
School, Grantham, he worked on the farm at Woolsthorpe before entering Trinity College, Cambridge. Driven home by the Plague in 1665

Woolsthorpe Manor where Isaac Newton was born.

he evolved here the theory of gravity, prompted by the fall of an apple in the orchard.

Nine items of graffiti preserved around the house have been attributed to Newton. They include a post windmill, a church, a bird, a man and a geometrical design of squares and triangles. Over the fireplace in the bedchamber a marble tablet quotes Alexander Pope's epitaph:

> "Nature and nature's laws lay hid in night;
> God said Let Newton be! and all was light".

In the study across the landing is a reconstruction of his experiment with spectrum and prism, which probably took place here. Other artefacts include a celestial globe, telescope and a copy of his monumental *Principia Mathematica*, outlining the laws of motion.

A pewter death mask hangs above the fireplace. Newton died on 20th March, 1727 while addressing the Royal Society, and is buried in Westminster Abbey.

Places of Interest in the Neighbourhood
6. Sheltered Stocks (Witham)
11. An Auctioneer's Epitaph (Corby Glen)

The imposing front of Folkingham's House of Correction.

13 A House of Correction

Position: Folkingham, on the A15 midway between Sleaford and
Bourne.
O.S. Map: Grantham, Sheet No. 130
Map Ref: TF 075/335
Access: Off the Market Place and about two hundred yards down
Billingborough Road. The House stands on the left on rising ground.

The years after the Napoleonic Wars were troubled by widespread
poverty and hardship. Gradually regional Houses of Correction were
set up for less serious malefactors – poachers, trespassers, vagrants
(troublesome since Tudor times), hooligans at fairs, thieves, drunkards,
fallen women and the like.

The Folkingham 'House', begun in 1808 and enlarged in 1825, was
built on the site of a former castle bailey whose moat is still visible. Only
the handsome front portico now remains, stone-faced with three bays.
Once it accommodated the turnkey and the governor's horses and carriage. The regime was tough, with only bread and gruel being served for
the first week. For men it involved stone-breaking and the treadwheel.
Women were required to do laundry, cleaning, knitting and picking
oakum. This 'House', like others nationwide, was closed in 1878 when a
radical shake-up of local institutions was effected by the Prisons Act.

Immediately behind the Square, St. Andrew's Church has at its west
end a set of stocks and a whipping post.

Places of Interest in the Neighbourhood
15. A Jawbone Arch (Threekingham)

14 The Vicar's Sentry Box

Position: Quadring, seven miles north of Spalding on A152
O.S. Map: Boston and Spalding, Sheet No. 131
Map Ref: TF 225/341
Access: The Church of St. Margaret is detached from the main village, and is reached by a side road called Cross Gate.

A Georgian relic peculiar in Lincolnshire to the flatter hinterland of the Wash is the wooden hude or hudd, deriving perhaps from 'hood'. Standing about seven feet high it was placed, when rain threatened, at the head of the grave to shelter the vicar whilst he was conducting the burial service.

At Quadring the hudd stands in a corner near the entrance. There are seven panels and a large opening at the front. From church to church the style varies little, apart from the number of sides and the roof, which may be pointed, as at Friskney (TF 461/554) or curved, as at Deeping St. James (TF 157/096). At Donington (TF 207/359) the hudd stands, appropriately perhaps, beside a disused bier in the north-west corner. Another survives at Pinchbeck (TF 243/256).

Places of Interest in the Neighbourhood
10. The Pinchbeck Engine (Pinchbeck)
15. A Jawbone Arch (Threekingham)

The 'hudd' in Quadring Church.

15 A Jawbone Arch

Position: Threekingham
O.S. Map: Grantham, Sheet No. 130
Map Ref: TF 087/362
Access: Threekingham lies just south of the A52 Grantham-Donington Road. Turn down Water Lane to find the whalebone arch leading to Laundon Hall, once the home of the Craggs family.

Folk lore attributes the place-name to the site of a battle in about 869 between the Saxons and Danes, in which three Danish kings were slain. A more recent 19th century story tells of an ill-fated whaling expedition, in which a member of the locally renowned Craggs family took part. The expedition's destination and its outcome have been eroded over the years in the story's telling. But local opinion asserts that the

Threekingham's whalebone arch.

jawbones were later given to Craggs by other members of the expedition as a souvenir. Some restoration of the bones took place in 1985.

During the last century a number of arches were built from the skeletons of whales stranded on this east coast eg. at Barton on Humber, Cleethorpes, Little Ponton, but these have disappeared. Another arch survives, however, in Cinder Ash Park, Long Sutton (TF 435/230).

Places of Interest in the Neighbourhood
13. A House of Correction (Folkingham)
14. The Vicar's Sentry Box (Quadring)

The Angel and Royal, Grantham.

16 The Angel and Royal

Position: Grantham
O.S. Map: Grantham, Sheet No. 130
Map Ref: SK 915/355
Access: High Street, at the junction with Market Place.

Although little of the original fabric remains, this was a famous medieval hostelry, and one of England's oldest. Its cellars date from the thirteenth century; and the restaurant retains something of the character of a medieval banqueting hall.

The building was a hostel for the Knights Templars until their dissolution in 1312, when it was taken over by the Knights Hospitallers. Gradually it became a meeting place for merchants en route to local fairs and markets. Tucked between the top of the central archway and the oriel window is a stone angel carrying a crown. Nor is 'Royal' an empty claim. On either side of the arch are the carved heads of Edward III and Queen Philippa. King John held court here in 1213, whilst it was in what is now the Restaurant that Richard III authorised the death warrant of the treacherous 2nd Duke of Buckingham. Charles I was also a visitor in 1633, but despite all these associations, it was not until after the visit of the Prince of Wales in 1866 that 'Royal' was added to 'Angel'.

Places of Interest in the Neighbourhood
17. A Chained Library (Grantham)

17 A Chained Library

Position: Grantham
O.S. Map: Grantham, Sheet No. 130
Map Ref: SK 915/356
Access: St Wulfram's Church lies off the High Street, via Vine Street
and Swine Street. It is necessary to make an appointment with the
Curator.

In 1598 the Rev. Francis Trigge, Rector of Welbourn, gave £100 for a
small library of books to be bought for the benefit of the clergy
and literate laity of Grantham. About 250 of the original volumes
remain. They include Bibles sermons, medical works, natural history,
law and theology. There are works by Lanfranc, Duns Scotus, Aquinas
and Peter Lombard. As if to demonstrate a late Tudor ecumenical
spirit, tomes of Lutheran and Calvinist preaching sit alongside Catholic
apologetics, attacks on papistry and refutations of Protestantism.

The books are displayed on three sets of shelves, many with their
spines at the back and the titles on the fore-edges of the leaves. We may
think it odd that such an erudite collection should ever have had to be
chained down against theft. Yet these books were always rare, and their
scholarly antiquity makes them priceless. Eighty-three chains remain.
One end is clasped to the top left-hand corner of each book, the other to
a ring which slides along a horizontal rod between the shelves. The
book could thus be lifted down but not removed.

Although this was never, in the normal sense, a public library, it is
thought that the Trigge collection was the first in England to be established outside a college or school.

Places of Interest in the Neighbourhood
16 The Angel and Royal (Grantham)

18 Eight Sails to the Wind

Position: Heckington, six miles east of Sleaford on the A17
O.S. Map: Grantham, Sheet No. 130
Map Ref: TF 144/435
Access: Station Road, by the railway. From Easter – September the mill is open from 2.00-4.30 p.m.; and from October-March, on Sunday afternoons.

For centuries Lincolnshire has been the 'land of the windmill'. But of the 900 surviving into the mid-nineteenth century, fewer than 200 remained by 1923, only half of them in working order. By 1953 only six were left.

The original five-sailed mill built here in 1830 suffered serious storm damage in 1890. An eight-sailed cap was acquired from the Tuxford Mill in Boston and grafted on to the reduced shell. Eight new sails enabled the mill to continue until 1942. Since 1953 this stately 59 feet high tower and much of the original machinery have been conserved by the County Council and Friends of Heckington Mill. Wind permitting, flour is ground for visitors on summer week-ends.

Eight sails are comparatively rare even in Lincolnshire, and Heckington is the only survivor. The even number of sails meant that if one was disabled, the sail opposite could be removed, and the mill could still function.

Places of Interest in the Neighbourhood
15. A Jawbone Arch (Threekingham)
25. Mud and Stud (Billinghay)

For illustration see Frontispiece.

19 In the Shadow of the Stump

Position: Boston
O.S. Map: Boston and Spalding, Sheet No. 131
Map Ref: TF 336/442
Access: The enormous tower of the Church of St. Botolph, by the River Witham, is easily identified.

Standing 272 feet high and a regional landmark, this slim majestic lantern tower, built during the fourteenth and fifteenth centuries, often reminds visitors of the belfry at Bruges. A direct continental link, located at the west end of the north aisle, is the black marble gravestone with an engraved portrait of Wisselus Smalenburg, a Hanseatic wool merchant of Munster who died here in 1340. At the base of the tower is a monument to five Boston men who became Governors of Massachusetts, where there is, of course, a namesake city. On a nearby door is a rare twelfth century sanctuary knocker – older than the Church – which once gave sanctuary access to refugees from the law. Other noteworthy features include the pulpit of 1612; a superb collection of boss carvings; and sixty well-preserved misericord carvings in the stalls, one of which shows a wolf in clerical dress preaching to geese, with a fox waiting.

Boston's historical importance owes much to the River Witham, on whose banks the Stump stands. By the thirteenth century Boston ranked second only to London as a port, thanks mainly to the Hanseatic trade in wool and wines. In 1369 it replaced Lincoln as the staple town for wool, hides and tin. The town developed many links with the Pilgrim Fathers. Two early Puritans, William Brewster and William Bradford, were imprisoned in the Guildhall in 1607, and their cells may be visited.

Within a short distance of the Stump there are many worthwhile stopping points. The statue just outside the precincts is of Herbert Ingram (1811-1860), another son of Boston, founder of the *Illustrated London News* and a tireless campaigner for gas lighting, piped water and the railway. A plaque on the front of the adjacent inn, Martha's Vineyard, marks the site of the birth of John Foxe (1516-1587), author of the celebrated *Book of Martyrs.* Just east of the market place are 'the lanes', like Strait Bargate and Wormgate, which formed part of the town's medieval grid pattern. Off the Green and behind the Horncastle Road is the five-sailed Maud Foster Windmill, the tallest working mill in England.

Places of Interest in the Neighbourhood
20. A Roof-Top Curiosity (Freiston)

36

20 A Roof-Top Curiosity

Position: Freiston, between Boston and the Wash
O.S. Map: Boston and Spalding, Sheet No. 131
Map Ref: TF 398/437
Access: At the T-junction by the parish church turn left along Shore
Road. At the next junction White Loaf Hall is signposted left, and is the
large white farmhouse at the end of the lane.

White Loaf Hall is a large brick and slate farmhouse, parts of which go
back to Tudor times. It was once a monastery, and even perhaps
a prison. Some mullioned windows and a fine staircase have been
retained, and architecturally it is distinguished by a pair of splendid
white stepped gables, one of which is surmounted by a stone shaped like
a loaf of bread and bearing the letters WLH and the date 1614. It is
claimed that in Jacobean times, the first loaf of white bread ever to
appear in England was baked by monks. Hitherto, brown bread had
been the staple diet.

Places of Interest in the Neighbourhood
19. In the Shadow of the Stump (Boston)

White Loaf Hall gable and Loaf, Freiston.

21 Obelisk Milestones

Position: Normanton, on the A607, seven miles west of Sleaford
O.S. Map: Grantham, Sheet No. 130
Map Ref: SK 948/464
Access: Village street, west side.

Milestones go back to the Roman era, and the rare survivors are now in museums. They did not re-appear until the eighteenth century when turnpike trusts were required to establish signposts and mileage

The milestone at Normanton.

markers within their area. Victorian local enterprise sometimes called for enlarged wayside monuments, such as the obelisk erected about 1870 at Normanton. It stands about twelve feet tall, with a water trough at its base and the remains of a pump behind. The inscription gives the mileages to Lincoln (18), Grantham (7) and London (117).

A similar obelisk, though rather older (c. 1840) is to be found on the Main Street at Belton (SK 928/395).

Places of Interest in the Neighbourhood
22. Byard's Leap
23. The Templars' Temple (Temple Bruer)
24. The Soldier Who Held Every Rank (Welbourn)

Horseshoes at Byard's Leap.

22 Byard's Leap

Position: Just south-west of RAF Cranwell, at the junction of the A17 and B6403 (A1)
O.S. Map: Grantham, Sheet No. 130
Map Ref: TF 990/493
Access: In front of the cafe and garage.

Centuries ago, according to legend, people living on Ancaster Heath suffered many privations. Crops failed and cattle died. It seemed that the fates were hostile. When an ugly old witch and her inevitable black cat took up residence in a local hovel, a sufficient scapegoat was to hand.

Big Jim, local knight-errant, was willing to do battle, but doubted the staying power of his horse, Byard, now of failing sight and wearied limbs. Gathering a number of likely horses around a pond, Big Jim threw in a stone and was agreeably surprised when Byard was the only one to rear in excitement. So he mounted, and shouting challenges, made for the hovel. Out and upwards leaped the witch, spiked-boots, vicious claws and all, landing squarely behind the rider, and immediately digging in her spikes and claws. Byard, sorely tormented, roared, reared and made a prodigious leap. Meg fell off. The knight turned, dismounted and swiftly despatched her.

The hoof marks are still there, represented by four horseshoes fenced off by the car park. Over a hundred yards away, across the road, is Byard's Leap mounting block. Between the two, partly hidden in the shrubbery, is another set of four horseshoes. Thus, a persistent story is remembered by a precise geographical location!

Places of Interest in the Neighbourhood
21. Obelisk Milestones (Normanton)
23. The Templars' Temple (Temple Bruer)
24. The Soldier Who Held Every Rank (Welbourn)

23 The Templars' Temple

Position: Temple Bruer, six miles north-west of Sleaford
O.S. Map: Lincoln, Sheet No. 121
Map Ref: TF 006/537
Access: From the A15, it is situated about two miles down the
Welbourn road. The Temple Bruer road takes longer.

Set in a delightful garden near to farm buildings, this fifty-one feet
high tower is an unexpected feature of an open heath. It is called the
'Templum de la Bruere', temple of the heath, and is all that remains of a
church of the Order of Knights Templar, established in about 1185 in
imitation of the Church of the Holy Sepulchre in Jerusalem.

Early in the twelfth century bands of Western European templars,
based in Jerusalem, offered protection to Christian pilgrims making
their way to the Holy Land. Such an organisation needed money,
volunteers, influence. Lincolnshire preceptories were established at Wil-
loughton and Aslackby as well as at Temple Bruer. Although wealth
collected in the county was channelled to Jerusalem, the temple also
contributed to the growth of the village.

Unfortunately, rumours of heresy and vice hardened into charges. In
1308 members of the Order were arrested and imprisoned in Lincoln.
Similar sequestrations were made in other parts of England. The Order
of Knights Hospitallers took over the Templars' protective role and
mounted a Crusade against the Turks. At the dissolution, Henry VIII
gave Temple Bruer to his brother-in-law, Charles Brandon, Duke of
Suffolk. Gradually the church buildings fell into ruins.

The tower is now under the guardianship of the County Council.
Inside, the rib-vaulted ground floor (perhaps once a chapel) has an
elaborate wall arcade with foliage capitals. It is possible to climb to an
empty chamber via the winding staircase. The pyramidal roof was
added during the early years of the twentieth century.

Places of Interest in the Neighbourhood
21. Obelisk Milestones (Normanton)
22. Byard's Leap
24. The Soldier who Held every Rank (Welbourn)

The tower at Temple Bruer.

24 The Soldier who Held every Rank

Position: Welbourn, nine miles south of Lincoln, just off the A607
O.S. Map: Lincoln, Sheet No. 121
Map Ref: SK 968/546
Access: No. 16 The Green and the Church of St. Chad may be found without difficulty in this small community.

A simple plaque on a terraced cottage in Welbourn records that this was the birthplace of Sir William Robertson. Born in 1860, Robertson was one of seven children and attended the local school. He was befriended by the rector who found him a job as a gardener. Whilst working at Deene Park, Northamptonshire, he saw paintings and memorabilia relating to the Earl of Cardigan, hero of the Charge of the Light Brigade in the Crimean War in 1854.

Thus inspired, William Robertson took the Queen's shilling and became a trooper in the 16th Lancers. During the next eight years he climbed steadily through the ranks, becoming a sergeant-major in 1885. Undaunted by the well-bred rivalry of ex-public school men, Robertson sought a commission and became the first ranker to pass through Staff College. Twenty-two years later, after experience in many parts of the world, he returned as Commandant, with the rank of Major-General. During the First World War he became Chief of the General Staff; and at the close of hostilities, Commander-in-Chief of the Rhine Army. Shortly afterwards he retired with a baronetcy and the rank of Field Marshal. It was appropriate that he should unveil the Memorial Cross, near the south door of the Church, to the eleven Welbourn villagers who died on the battlefields of France. On the north wall of the Church an armorial stone headed 'Fight the Good Fight' is dedicated to Field Marshal Sir William Robert Robertson, Bt., GGB, GCMG, GCVO, DSO, DCL (Oxon.), LL D. (Cantab) ... of "indomitable energy, resource, skill and judgment". He died on 12th February, 1933 and is buried in Brookwood Cemetery, four miles west of Dorking in Surrey.

Places of Interest in the Neighbourhood
21. Obelisk Milestones (Normanton)
22. Byard's Leap
23. The Templars' Temple (Temple Bruer)

25 Mud and Stud

Position: Billinghay, eight miles north-east of Sleaford on the A153
O.S. Map: Lincoln, Sheet No. 121
Map Ref: TF 157/549
Access: Turn off the northern side of the A153 for the village. The cottage is located between the Church and the Golden Cross Inn.

Until late medieval times mud and stud were common building materials. Mud was earth, puddled with chopped straw, ashes, manure and lime – even nuts and acorns. Studs were the main wooden posts, oak where possible, with a strong foundation of padstones. Laths of hazel, ash or willow were nailed to form a lattice which was then liberally covered with layers of the mud. The walls were smoothed and allowed to dry, limewash (lime plus tallow or linseed and water) was applied and a thatched roof added to provide a waterproof, cheap and relatively durable dwelling.

This former vicarage is an intriguing restoration. Built about 1650 it served as a vicarage until 1724. Originally it had two rooms and a

Billinghay's old vicarage.

central fireplace with a smoke hood. The brick chimney was added later, as was the loft. Parts of the front wall show clearly the mud and stud construction.

Other mud and stud dwellings may be seen at Mareham le Fen (TF 277/61O) where the Royal Oak Inn, thatched and whitewashed, carries the date 1473; Withern Cottage, reconstructed at Skegness Church Farm Museum and dating from the time of Charles II (TF 556/635) whilst at Thimbleby, just west of Horncastle, there is a row of three sixteenth century cottages just below the church (TF 239/700).

Places of Interest in the Neighbourhood
26. Fortress or Mansion? (Tattershall)
27. Horological Oddities (Coningsby)

Tattershall Castle Keep.

26 Fortress or Mansion?

Position: Tattershall
O.S. Map: Skegness, Sheet No. 122
Map Ref: TF 212/576
Access: The Castle, which lies on the south side of the A153 in the village, opens daily from Easter to October, and during the afternoons from November to March.

This unique six-storeyed medieval brick building was the creation of Ralph Cromwell, Lord High Treasurer of England who had fought at Agincourt in 1415. The surviving tower with octagonal corner turrets and ornate battlements was built from local bricks (probably Stixwould) on the site of an earlier fortification. There is also a guardhouse, together with the bases of two round towers, and the large inner moat is well preserved.

Following Cromwell's death in 1452 the keep was occupied by the Earls of Lincoln until about 1700. Two centuries of decline then followed, ending when four splendid fifteenth century fireplaces were removed for shipping to the United States. At this point, in 1911, a former Viceroy of India, Lord Curzon of Kedleston intervened and bought the Castle from the owning syndicate. At enormous personal cost he had it restored, fireplaces and all, and opened it to the public in 1914. When he died in 1925 he bequeathed it to the National Trust.

Cromwell had believed in solidity. At the base the walls are twenty feet thick. Each storey had a great stateroom. On the second floor the south-west turret contains a former dovecote with round holes and perches for some 260 birds. In the south-east turret the staircase winds to a height of 110 feet. From the parapet walk may be seen, on a clear day, Boston Stump (TF 336/442), Lincoln Cathedral (SK 978/718) and New York (TF 247/550) a village four miles away.

Places of Interest in the Neighbourhood
25. Mud and Stud (Billinghay)
27. Horological Oddities (Coningsby)

27 Horological Oddities

Position: Coningsby
O.S. Map: Skegness, Sheet No. 122
Map Ref: TF 223/580
Access: St. Michael's Parish Church is on the A153 in the middle of the village.

In earlier centuries many public clocks had only one hand. Here on the east side of this fifteenth century church tower is a survivor thought to be from the early 1600's. With a diameter of 16½ feet, it is probably the largest one-handed clock face in Britain.

The clock has two further unusual features. The pendulum, swinging every two seconds, is removed from the main mechanism but linked by a rod; and the striking apparatus is driven by two large stone weights, suspended on steel wire ropes, that require daily winding.

The clock's red centre and blue circumference are no accident. Coningsby and the Royal Air Force are proudly bonded. Inside the Church are many RAF memorabilia, including a Dutch flag recalling the heroism of Jacoba Maria Pulskens who helped many British aircrew to escape during the War.

At the end of a winding lane through Hameringham (TF 31O/673) five miles south-east of Horncastle, All Saints Church has a much smaller, though intriguing, timepiece inside. When long sermons were common, hour glasses were placed by the pulpit to remind the preacher not to encroach on eternity. Nowadays, few hour glasses remain, and this one is a rarity. It is attached to a bracket on the side of the Jacobean pulpit.

Places of Interest in the Neighbourhood
26. Fortress or Mansion? (Tattershall)
30. The Dambusters' Memorial (Woodhall Spa)
31. The Flicks in the Sticks (Woodhall Spa)
32. Winding Gear and Bath Chairs (Woodhall Spa)

Coningsby's one-handed clock.

28 Friend of the Famous

Position: Wainfleet
O.S. Map: Skegness, Sheet No. 122
Map Ref: TF 499/599
Access: From the Market Place, St. John's Street leads straight to Magdalen School, left.

William Patten was born at Wainfleet in about 1395. After early schooling in the town and in Winchester, he went to Oxford, changing the 'Patten' for 'Waynflete'. Claiming the scholarly attention of Cardinal Beaufort, he became headmaster of Winchester, where his reputation attracted, amongst others, Henry VI. The royal patronage soon translated him to Eton, where he became head of the new foundation. In 1447 Waynflete succeeded his old mentor, Beaufort, as Bishop of Winchester. From this powerful position he founded a new Oxford college, Magdalen, and went on to become Lord Chancellor.

Following his resignation, Waynflete decided to establish a school in his home town – Magdalen College School – originally for seven boys to work for places in his Oxford College. The mellow redbrick building was finished in 1484. Two years later he died and was buried in Winchester Cathedral.

Inevitably, over five hundred years there have been changes. By the middle of the eighteenth century the School had grown in numbers, and was providing for ordinary boys and girls. But by 1877 the pupils on roll were down to three. A reconstruction on grammar school lines lasted until 1933. During the Second World War the building was used by army personnel, becoming a school again between 1951 and 1966. Since 1968 it has been used as a County Library, and has Scheduled Ancient Monument status. Behind the card desk is a richly crafted tapestry linking the centuries 1484 – 1984.

Places of Interest in the Neighbourhood
29. That Jolly Fisherman (Skegness)

The front of Magdelen College School, Wainfleet.

29 That Jolly Fisherman

Position: Skegness
O.S. Map: Skegness, Sheet No. 122 ˙
Map Ref: TF 571/633
Access: Tower Esplanade, facing the sea, looking right.

The young London commercial artist, John Hassall, had never even been to Skegness when he painted his famous poster of the fisherman bounding along the beach. It was commissioned in 1908 by the Great Northern Railway Company to advertise day trips to 'Skeggy' from London's King's Cross, and earned him twelve guineas and a kind of immortality. With its laconic welcome, "Skegness is so bracing", it has popularised the resort to the present day.

If one looks left from the Esplanade into Compass Gardens, there is a statue of the Fisherman, presented by the mayor in 1989.

Places of Interest in the Neighbourhood
28. Friend of the Famous (Wainfleet)

The Jolly Fisherman.

30 The Dambusters' Memorial

Position: Woodhall Spa
O.S. Map: Skegness, Sheet No. 122
Map Ref: TF 196/634
Access: The Royal Square is close by the main crossroads.

The Memorial, in the shape of a miniature dam, was erected in 1987. Although the Lancasters that flew in the famous Dambusters' Raid had taken off from RAF Scampton, 617 Squadron had transferred to Woodhall Spa in 1943, and the Petwood Hotel became the officers' mess. The hotel bar room contains a lot of interesting memorabilia; and in the grounds are the remains of a bouncing bomb.

In the spring of 1943 many low level practice runs were made at Freiston Shore, east of Boston, and over the Derwent Reservoir in Derbyshire by Wing Commander Guy Gibson's chosen crews. It was essential for the 'bouncing bombs', designed by Dr. Barnes Wallis, to be

The Memorial to 617 Squadron, Woodhall Spa.

delivered from a height of only sixty feet. But the spotlights slung under each aircraft to fix the required height vastly increased everyone's vulnerability. After his own bomb failed, Gibson deliberately attracted enemy fire so as to give his colleagues maximum room for manoeuvre. The destruction of the Mohne and Eder Dams in the early hours of 17th May 1943 was one of the most imaginative, skilful and heroic exploits of the War. Eight of the nineteen Lancasters failed to return to base. Thirty-two decorations were awarded, Gibson receiving the Victoria Cross. In September 1944 this gallant officer was reported missing after a raid on Munchen Gladbach.

The centre-piece of this magnificent and moving Memorial lists the eight theatres of the European War in which the Dambusters operated. On either side are three arches inscribed with a total of two hundred and four British, Canadian, Australian and New Zealand airmen who gave their lives for our freedom.

Places of Interest in the Neighbourhood
26. Fortress or Mansion? (Tattershall)
27. Horological Oddities (Coningsby)
31. The Flicks in the Sticks (Woodhall Spa)
32. Winding Gear and Bath Chairs (Woodhall Spa)

31 The Flicks in the Sticks

Position: Woodhall Spa
O.S. Map: Skegness, Sheet No. 122
Map Ref: TF 197/636
Access: The Kinema is situated in woodland off the north side of the Broadway. It opens daily, as a rule.

This picturesque building was originally a cricket pavilion for Petwood House, but in 1922 was converted by Captain Cole Allport into the Pavilion Cinema. During the Second World War visitors in the armed forces dubbed it 'the flicks in the sticks'.

Unusually, it uses rear projection and retains its original Compton theatre organ, which rises from the floor to entertain the audience during the interval. The now re-named Kinema deliberately cultivates an old-world atmosphere – although the films are up-to-date.

Places of Interest in the Neighbourhood
26. Fortress or Mansion? (Tattershall)
27. Horological Oddities (Coningsby)
30. The Dambusters' Memorial (Woodhall Spa)
32. Winding Gear and Bath Chairs (Woodhall Spa)

Woodhall Spa's rural picture-house.

32 Winding Gear and Bath Chairs

Position: Woodhall Spa
O.S. Map: Skegness, Sheet No. 122
Map Ref: TF 197/636
Access: In the wooded area off the north side of Broadway, approached via Coronation Road or Spa Road.

At first sight it is surprising to find a 'Welcome' sign to Woodhall Spa portraying colliery winding gear; some maps, moreover, show 'Coal Pit Wood'. The story goes back to 1811 when an Old Bolingbroke man, John Parkinson, persuaded himself that coal lay beneath these heaths. After some preliminary borings he was encouraged by a number of miners who deliberately introduced 'black diamond' samples. But by 1817 the shaft was flooded and Parkinson was bankrupt.

Some years later Thomas Hotchkin felt that applications of the shaft water were helping his gout. Chemical analysis confirmed that the water was rich in bromine and iodine. By 1830 he had built a bath house over the shaft and was inviting rheumatism sufferers to take the waters. For Woodhall Spa, as the site now became, the Victorian era was one of enormous expansion. From 1855 the railways provided links with Boston and Lincoln and thousands of visitors came to drink the waters. In 1887 the Bath and Pump Rooms were refurbished by the city architect of Bath. The Royal Hydro Hotel, Winter Gardens, a bandstand and donkey-drawn bath-chairs became part of the fashionable social scene.

But after 1918 there was a steady decline, accentuated by the loss of two major hotels – the Victoria (another of Hotchkin's investments) by fire in 1920, and the Royal Hydro by enemy action in 1943. But the old Spa building lingers on, despite a partial collapse of the well shaft and the pump room chimney in 1983. With its ever-spreading red creeper over the brick and stucco, and its ample reception and treatment rooms and corridors deserted, it looks forlorn, a sad period piece. But many visitors come to see it, and it remains a curiosity.

Places of Interest in the Neighbourhood
26. Fortress or Mansion? (Tattershall)
27. Horological Oddities (Coningsby)
30. The Dambusters' Memorial (Woodhall Spa)
31. The Flicks in the Sticks (Woodhall Spa)

33 An Inland Lighthouse

Position: 6 ½ miles south-east of Lincoln, beside the A15. Despite its name, Dunston Pillar lies some three miles west of Dunston village
O.S. Map: Lincoln, Sheet No. 121
Map Ref: TF 008/620
Access: About two hundred yards north of the B1202 to Metheringham lies the opening to the Pillar.

Dunston Pillar stands ninety-two feet tall and was erected in 1751 by Sir Francis Dashwood MP, of Nocton Hall. For many years it was surmounted by a fifteen foot beacon as a guide to travellers crossing the heath, then a notorious haunt of footpads. Knowing Sir Francis as the founder of the Hell Fire Club, some credulous locals thought that the beacon fire was indeed drawn from Hell! A story is told of the postboy who, when advised to keep the light to his right, did so by driving round and round until the approaching dawn persuaded him of his mistake.

In 1810 the beacon lantern was removed by order of the Earl of Buckingham, and replaced by a statue of King George III in celebration of his Golden Jubilee. It cost the life of a mason, John Wilson, who fell to his death while erecting it, and in 1940 it was removed as a danger to low-flying aircraft from Coleby Heath. The remains of the statue may be seen by the bath-house in the grounds of Lincoln Castle.

The original wording on the Pillar has been badly eroded, and little of the inscription can be made out apart from 'AD MDCCLI' and 'KING GEORGE THE THIRD'.

Places of Interest in the Neighbourhood
30. The Dambusters' Memorial (Woodhall Spa)
31. The Flicks in the Sticks (Woodhall Spa)
32. Winding Gear and Bath Chairs (Woodhall Spa)

34 'Time Honour'd Lancaster' and Son

Position: Old Bolingbroke, three miles west of Spilsby
O.S. Map: Skegness, Sheet No. 122
Map Ref: TF 349/648
Access: From the centre of the village, pass the Black Horse Inn and
walk a short distance along the lane. The second gate on the right opens
to visitors.

It was at Old Bolingbroke Castle in 1366 that Blanche, wife and cousin
of John of Gaunt, gave birth to a future King of England, Henry IV.
Enough of the walls of Old Bolingbroke still stand for the hexagonal
outline to be seen, and much of the moat also remains. The Castle, built
by Ranulph de Blundevill between 1220 and 1230, was acquired by the
House of Lancaster in 1311 and John of Gaunt, fourth son of Edward
III, was the last of the dynasty to live there.

Ancient arches at Old Bolingbroke.

Henry's reign (1399-1413) was short but eventful. Even Shakespeare needed Two Parts to describe the shifting alliances and plots that characterise his years on the throne, also recording Bolingbroke's long-held belief about the ordained place of his death:

"It hath been prophesied to me many years,
I should not die but in Jerusalem".

Interestingly, he expired in the Jerusalem Chamber of the Palace of Westminster.

Not too surprisingly, perhaps, the Castle was a Royalist stronghold during the Civil War, until the débâcle at Winceby in 1643 (See No. 40). By order of the Parliamentary authorities it was then partly demolished, and the stone was used for local building. Some excavations took place during the 1960's, and the site is maintained by English Heritage.

Places of Interest in the Neighbourhood
35. The Man Who Ate His Boots (Spilsby)
36. The Lion Gateway (Scrivelsby)
37. Philip's Mill (Hagworthingham)

35 The Man Who Ate His Boots

Position: Spilsby
O.S. Map: Skegness, Sheet No. 122.
Map Ref: TF 402/661
Access: Spilsby lies on the A16 Louth to Boston road. The market square is situated to the east of St. James's Church and the main crossroads.

A plaque in the wall of the High Street bakery marks the 1786 birthplace of Sir John Franklin, the youngest of twelve children. Fascinated by visits to the coast, he joined the Navy at the age of fourteen, and took part in the Battle of Copenhagen. His skills in maritime surveying were fostered by his distinguished cousin, Matthew Flinders, during their circumnavigation of Australia, 1801-3. While still a teenage signaller he fought the French at Trafalgar.

Gradually he grew interested in the search for a North West Passage to the Indies via the Arctic coast of Canada. In 1819 he was invited to command the first overland expedition with the specific task of improving the cartography of the rivers and coastline of the North West Territories. When food supplies ran out, Franklin and his companions survived on dead animals, lichens – and by eating chewed boot leather! A further expedition to the Mackenzie River basin earned Franklin the Geographical Society's gold medal and a knighthood. There followed periods of service in the Mediterranean and as Lieutenant Governor of Van Dieman's Land (Tasmania), where he achieved much.

In 1845, with his sixtieth birthday looming, Franklin sailed again for the North West passage on what was to be his last voyage. His ships, the *Erebus* and *Terror* were last sighted on 26th July by an Aberdeen whaler off Lancaster Sound north of Baffin Island. His aim was to negotiate the channel between Victoria Island and the mainland, and thus enter the Arctic Ocean. When nothing further was seen or heard, a relief ship set out in 1847.

Lady Franklin never gave up hope. An expedition of 1859 found a cairn at Port Victory with the vital log book showing that the Passage had indeed been discovered. His ships had been abandoned in April 1848, entombed in the ice pack. Franklin had died on 11th June, 1847 but his body was never found.

Spilsby Market Square is dominated by a bronze statue of Sir John Franklin, whilst his memorial in Westminster Abbey was written by his nephew, Alfred Lord Tennyson.

"Not here: the white North hath thy bones, and thou,
Heroic Sailor Soul,
Art passing on thy happier voyage now,
Toward no Earthly Pole".

Places of Interest in the Neighbourhood
34. 'Time Honour'd Lancaster' and Son (Old Bolingbroke)
36. The Lion Gateway (Scrivelsby)
37. Philip's Mill (Hagworthingham)

The Franklin Memorial in Spilsby market place.

36 The Lion Gateway

Position: Scrivelsby is situated about 2½ miles south of Horncastle
O.S. Map: Skegness, Sheet No. 122
Map Ref: TF 266/662
Access: The Gateway is beside the B1183 to Boston.

The Lion Gateway was built about 1530 by Sir Robert Dymoke, King's Champion at the coronations of Richard III, 1483; Henry VII in 1485; and Henry VIII in 1509. The appointment of Royal Champion appears to have descended from Norman times, for Robert Marmion was rewarded by William the Conqueror with Scrivelsby Manor, and his family forebears had been Champions to the Dukes of Normandy. The Marmions were eventually succeeded by the Dymokes, and since 1350 the hereditary title has remained with the Dymoke family of Scrivelsby Court. The Lion worthily symbolises the dignity of this ancient Office.

During the coronation banquet in Westminster Hall it was the Champion's duty to enter in full armour on a suitably caparisoned white horse, to throw down a gauntlet and challenge to mortal combat anyone denying the new monarch's right to the throne. Such a challenge was, of course, never accepted. The monarch drank from a gold cup in thanks to the Champion, who received it as his fee and souvenir. The last occasion when the full ritual was carried out was in 1821 at the coronation of George IV. At the coronations of Edward VII, George V and George VI the Royal Champion carried the Standard of England; and in 1953, at the Coronation of Queen Elizabeth, the Union Standard was carried in the procession in Westminster Abbey by Lt. Col. J.L.M. Dymoke, MBE.

Places of Interest in the Neighbourhood
38. Bulls and Horses (Horncastle)
39. The Long Drop (Horncastle)
40. Thirteen Scythe Blades (Horncastle)

The Lion Gateway, Scrivelsby.

37 Philip's Mill

Position: Hagworthingham
O.S. Map: Skegness, Sheet No. 122
Map Ref: TF 358/704
Access: Stockwith Mill is situated down the Harrington Road on the eastern side of the village. lt is open from 10.00am. to 6.00pm. from April to September.

This seventeenth century water mill is set in a beautiful rural location by the River Lymn, only a short distance from Somersby Rectory where Alfred Lord Tennyson was born in 1809. Although critical opinion has doubted whether "The Brook" was intended by the poet to mean solely the Somersby stream, there seems to be agreement that only Stockwith could be linked to the memorable lines -
   "Till last by Philip's farm I flow
   To join the brimming river".

Places of Interest in the Neighbourhood
34. 'Time Honour'd Lancaster' and Son (Old Bolingbroke)
35. The Man Who Ate His Boots (Spilsby)
36. The Lion Gateway (Scrivelsby)

Stockwith Mill, Hagworthingham.

38 Bulls And Horses

Position: Horncastle
O.S. Map: Skegness, Sheet No. 122
Map Ref: TF 264/694
Access: The Bull Ring lies to the east of the Market Place.

In this busy market town horses are an uncommon sight. Yet the Bull Ring was once the heart of the August Horse Fair, lasting for three weeks in its eighteenth century heyday. On the old Bull Hotel we can still see the arch beneath which the mail coach from Boston clattered in every morning. Next door, on the front of Lloyd's Bank, is a plaque recalling the ancient Horse Fair. Opposite is the whitewashed King's Head Inn, the town's one remaining mud and stud building. Much has changed since George Borrow visited the Fair in 1825, describing people and events in several chapters of his *Romany Rye* but much of its old atmosphere remains.

The Horse Fair began with the granting of the town Charter in 1229 and lasted for seven centuries. In its heyday agents for monarchs, princes and landed gentry jostled with cavalry men, ostlers, waggoners, farmers, dealers, company representatives for coal and lead mines, as well as thieves and footpads. Literally thousands of horses were bought and sold, and there are many accounts of swindles, speedy cosmetic changes, imprudent first-time buyers .... yet many excellent bargains were struck.

The coming of the railway in 1855 signalled a major change. During the period of the Fair, something like a thousand animals per week were brought to Horncastle by the new 'iron horse'. But by the end of the First World War the Fair was in decline, all trading was done in a single day, and mostly for local farmers. The Fair was held for the last time in 1948.

Places of Interest in the Neighbourhood
36. The Lion Gateway (Scrivelsby)
39. The Long Drop (Horncastle)
40. Thirteen Scythe Blades (Horncastle)

39 The Long Drop

Position: Horncastle
O.S. Map: Skegness, Sheet No. 122
Map Ref: TF 257/695
Access: No. 6, Church Lane is alongside St. Mary's Church.

This small house in the middle of a terrace of brick and pantile houses was once a cobbler's shop. Eventually the proprietor took to advertising his profession 'Boot and Shoe Maker and Executioner,' for as the plaque explains, William Marwood was public executioner from 1872 to 1883. At the rear of the premises he perfected 'the long drop', experimenting with bags of corn and his preferred ropes of Italian silk hemp.

Swarthy and stocky of build, Marwood became a notorious showman, fond of displaying his powerful hands. At the annual Horse Fair he exhibited his ropes at sixpence a time. He delighted in a professional anecdote of a murderer's last request for a drink – granted with a rejoinder about the last drop but one.

A permanent self-advertisement is the white block inscribed "W.M. 1877" on a wall of his cottage, just round the corner in St. Mary's Square.

Amongst the last of his three hundred and fifty executions were the infamous Charles Peace and three Irishmen convicted of the Phoenix Park murders in Dublin. Marwood himself died of pneumonia in 1883 at the age of sixty-five. He was buried in an unmarked grave in the grounds of Holy Trinity Church on the Spilsby Road.

Places of Interest in the Neighbourhood
36. The Lion Gateway (Scrivelsby)
38. Bulls and Horses (Horncastle)
40. Thirteen Scythe Blades (Horncastle)

40 Thirteen Scythe Blades

Position: Horncastle
O.S. Map: Skegness, Sheet No. 122
Map Ref: TF 257/695
Access: St. Mary's Church is immediately behind the Market Square.

Above the arch in the Lady Chapel of St. Mary's Church are displayed thirteen scythe blades, found, according to tradition, following the Battle of Winceby, fought near here during the Civil War.

Royalist forces under Sir John Henderson clashed with those of Cromwell and Fairfax at Winceby in 1643. During the turmoil, Cromwell's horse fell beneath him and he was knocked down by Sir Ingram Hopton, who invited him to surrender. But Cromwell rose, took another horse from one of his men and inspired the Roundheads to fight on. They rapidly gained the upper hand, with much bloodshed, particularly in what came to be called Slash Hollow, north-west of the hamlet. Among the thousand or so victims was Hopton. Cromwell later chivalrously arranged for him to be buried with honours, and a colourful hatchment on the wall of the south aisle recalls the deed.

As a consequence of Winceby, the Cavalier retreat left Lincolnshire a Parliamentary County until the restoration of the monarchy in 1660. Hopton Street and Ingram Row remember a local leader who came close to despatching Old Noll.

There is, however, an alternative account, which says that these thirteen scythe blades may have been used during the Pilgrimage of Grace in 1536. No wonder Henry VIII called Lincolnshire "the most brute and beastlike shire" in his realm. Finally, this rebellion of some twenty thousand men led by Abbot Makarell of Barlings Abbey near Lincoln was ferociously suppressed.

Places of Interest in the Neighbourhood
36. The Lion Gateway (Scrivelsby)
38. Bulls and Horses (Horncastle)
39. The Long Drop (Horncastle)

41 Steep Hill

Position: Lincoln
O.S. Map: Lincoln, Sheet No. 121
Map Ref: SK 976/717
Access: Steep Hill links the 'uphill' area of the Cathedral and Castle with 'downhill' commerce and industry.

Be warned, Steep Hill lives up to its name! Noteworthy is the barrier halfway down, erected to deter anyone wishing to emulate a certain Colonel Sibthorpe who, for a bet, somehow drove down these cobbles in a coach and four and survived.

There are attractive buildings all the way, including some seventeenth and eighteenth century shop fronts. At the junction with Michaelgate is the Harlequin, of sixteenth century origin, formerly an inn, now an antiquarian bookshop. On the opposite side is Aaron's House, erroneously named, according to the plaque, but dating from the twelfth century when the wool trade made Lincoln prosperous. Further down on the left is Harding House, a sixteenth century merchant's house with a timber-framed upper storey, possibly used for weaving. On the lower slopes, where the hill widens, are two splendid examples of twelfth century domestic architecture. Jews House is associated with the legendary St. Hugh; and next door, Jews Court which may once have accommodated a synagogue – abandoned following the expulsion of the Jewish community from England in 1290 - has become the offices of the Society for Lincolnshire History and Archaeology.

It is difficult to think of a street that offers more antiquity, variety and curiosity – all against the incomparable backdrop of Lincoln Cathedral.

Places of Interest in the Neighbourhood
42. The Lincoln Imp (Lincoln)
43. That Rare Vellum Square (Lincoln)
44. Separation and Silence (Lincoln)
45. The Newport Arch (Lincoln)

Steep Hill perspectives, Lincoln.

70

42 The Lincoln Imp

Position: Lincoln
O.S. Map: Lincoln, Sheet No. 121
Map Ref: SK 977/718
Access: The Cathedral occupies a dominant position in the north centre of the city. The Angel Choir is at the east end of the building.

The Imp's features are common throughout the city, and Lincoln City Football Club is, of course, the Imps. Yet the original can be a little hard to find, even when you have tracked him down to the Cathedral.

It is extraordinary that so many accounts of how he came to be there involve the wind. For example, as Satan's representative he one day took shelter from it by entering the Cathedral, where he was promptly turned to stone. There is a more favoured traditional story. Soon after the Angel Choir was built, the Devil sent two Imps to create havoc. Blown to Lincoln by the wind, they were at first awestruck by the vast cathedral. One eventually decided to enter. But the wind, regretting its earlier cooperation, refused to blow him through the great west door. So the Imp flew in unaided, tore down the tapestries, threw books about the choir, broke candles, slammed doors, insulted the Bishop and teased the vergers and choristers. This brought the strongest protests from the Angels; and when the Imp threatened to pluck their feathers to make a bed, the smallest Angel turned him to stone.

He is located on the north side of the Angel Choir, second plinth from the end, between the arches. Grotesque, right leg crossed over left knee, there he sits, half human, half animal, leering at visitors as he has done for many centuries.

Places of Interest in the Neighbourhood
41. Steep Hill (Lincoln)
43. That Rare Vellum Square (Lincoln)
44. Separation and Silence (Lincoln)
45. The Newport Arch (Lincoln)

That legendary Lincoln Imp.

43 That Rare Vellum Square

Position: Lincoln
O.S. Map: Lincoln, Sheet No. 121
Map Ref: SK 977/718
Access: Lincoln Castle occupies a dominant position opposite the
Cathedral. The permanent Magna Carta exhibition is housed in the
red-brick complex adjacent to the former County Gaol.

Lincoln has a copy of the Magna Carta, so does Salisbury Cathedral,
and there are two more in the British Library, but few documents are
rarer – or of greater historical importance. Over forty original Charters
were drawn up for despatch to the counties, Lincoln's arriving in June
1215 with Bishop Hugh, who had been present at its signing at Run-
nymede. The Great Charter had been drawn up a fortnight previously
when King John had been obliged to come to terms with his disaffected
barons and church and civic leaders. Unlawful tax demands, quarrels
with the Pope and military defeat in France had brought England to the
brink of civil war, with the barons withdrawing their allegiance to the
king. There is another local connection: Stephen Langton, Archbishop
of Canterbury and instrumental in the drafting of the Charter, was
himself a Lincolnshire man, born at Langton by Wragby.

Magna Carta was England's first constitutional document, the cor-
nerstone of English civil rights and the rule of law. It became a
landmark in the continuing struggles over taxation, land rights and the
Royal Prerogative. About fifteen inches square, and made of calf-
skin, the Charter shows fifty-three lines of medieval Latin, not readily
decipherable by lay eyes. Yet its strongly asserted principles have
affected not only the course of English history, but have influenced
constitutional documents all over the world, especially the United
States.

Places of Interest in the Neighbourhood
41. Steep Hill (Lincoln)
42. The Lincoln Imp (Lincoln)
44. Separation and Silence (Lincoln)
45. The Newport Arch (Lincoln)

44 Separation and Silence

Position: Lincoln
O.S. Map: Lincoln, Sheet No. 121
Map Ref: SK 977/718
Access: Lincoln Castle is at the top of Castle Hill, opposite the Cathedral. The former County Gaol, in red-brick, stands to the left beyond the entrance.

Inside Lincoln's former County Gaol, which closed in 1878, is a unique survival of the Victorian 'separate system': the prison chapel. The semi-circular ranks of pew-boxes were high, individual, lockable and coffin-like – so that the prisoners could not see one another. Thus, their attention had to be focused on the chaplain preaching his sermon of repentance from a high central pulpit. On either side of the gangway the front seven seats were normally reserved for female prisoners. The back row was for those condemned to death.

Places of Interest in the Neighbourhood
41. Steep Hill (Lincoln)
42. The Lincoln Imp (Lincoln)
43. That Rare Vellum Square (Lincoln)
45. The Newport Arch (Lincoln)

Inside the Victorian Prison Chapel, Lincoln.

45 The Newport Arch

Position: Lincoln. This northern suburb of the city is Newport, from which the 'gate' takes its name
O.S. Map: Lincoln, Sheet No. 121
Map Ref: SK 976/730
Access: On Bailgate, north of the Cathedral.

The north gate of Roman Lindum still functions for something like its original purpose. The arch spans the main road, and hundreds of vehicles pass daily where chariots once were driven. To the west there was probably another arch with a pedestrian walk, mirroring the present remains. During the nineteen hundred years since the gate was built, the Street level has risen about eight feet, so the arch would have looked even more impressive.

Roman Lincoln began in the middle of the first century as a military garrison for the Ninth Legion. Public buildings, colonnaded streets, a water supply and road and canal communications were gradually established, whilst the great Roman road, Ermine Street, led from the Newport Arch to Winteringham, and beyond the Humber to York.

Places of Interest in the Neighbourhood
41. Steep Hill (Lincoln)
42. The Lincoln Imp (Lincoln)
43. That Rare Vellum Square (Lincoln)
44. Separation and Silence (Lincoln)

The Newport Arch, Lincoln.

46 A Gibbet Headpiece

Position: Doddington, three miles west of Lincoln
O.S. Map: Lincoln, Sheet No. 121
Map Ref: SK 899/701
Access: Doddington Hall is open to visitors from May-September on
Wednesday and Sunday afternoons.

This is certainly a macabre curiosity to find on the drawing room
mantlepiece of a stately home. Tommy Otter was a reluctant
bridegroom who had to be physically hauled to his nuptials at
Hykeham Church in 1805. On their way home from a quarrelsome
celebration that night at a local inn, Tommy Otter battered his bride to
death with a fence stake. Shortly afterwards he was arrested, with blood
on his sleeve, in another hostelry; and after standing trial he was
publicly hanged in March 1806. His body was suspended in irons from
a thirty foot gibbet erected at the end of Doddington Lane. This grisly
spectacle was nevertheless the occasion of many a social outing. The
following year it was noted that a blue tit was nesting in the jaw
bones. . .

Eventually the gibbet collapsed in a gale and the irons were removed
for safe keeping to the Hall, apparently by Edwin Jarvis, an antiquarian. For many years an odd rumour clung to the murder weapon.
On the anniversary of the murder the stake was wont to disappear from
its customary home at the Sun Inn, Saxilby, where Mrs. Otter's body
had first been brought. It was then re-laid at the scene of the crime, only
to be returned again to the inn. Finally it was burnt, by order of the
Bishop. Or so the story goes.

Curiosity seekers will be further intrigued to note that on the other
end of the mantelpiece is a scold's bridle.

Places of Interest in the Neighbourhood
41. Steep Hill (Lincoln)
42. The Lincoln Imp (Lincoln)
43. That Rare Vellum Square (Lincoln)
44. Separation and Silence (Lincoln)
45. The Newport Arch (Lincoln)

47 That Village Sign

Position: Saxilby
O.S. Map: Lincoln, Sheet No. 121
Map Ref: SK 894/754
Access: Village High Street.

This informative village sign was erected in 1984 in memory of Councillor Geoffrey Ford. Both sides appear to show similar features – a poacher, a church, a cow's head and four ears of wheat, and a boat.

These four vignettes illustrating key aspects of traditional life in Saxilby might well stand for the whole county. "The Lincolnshire Poacher" is, after all, sung with immense pride as the second national anthem. The county's churches are a glory and a delight. This is agricultural land par excellence, with a prodigious annual output of grain, beet and potatoes. As for boats, Saxilby is on the Fossdyke, and few counties have made greater use of their waterways.

Places of Interest in the Neighbourhood
46. A Gibbet Headpiece (Doddington)
48. Where the Fossdyke Ends (Torksey)

The graphic features of the Saxilby village street sign.

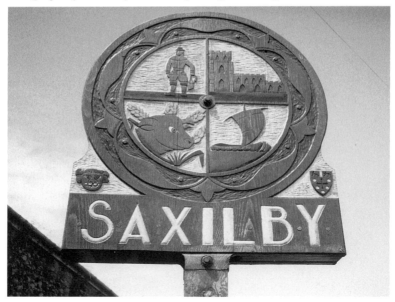

48 Where the Fossdyke Ends

Position: Torksey Lock
O.S. Map: Lincoln, Sheet No. 121
Map Ref: SK 838/781
Access: Alongside the A1133.

The Fossdyke was dug by first century Roman engineers (and slaves) to provide a canal linking the tidal Trent with Brayford Pool, Lincoln and the Witham. The Romans used this eleven mile waterway to carry food and military supplies. Torksey thus developed by the Trent junction. By the Domesday Survey of 1086 it was third in importance to Lincoln and Stamford, with its own mint and pottery. During the Middle Ages vast quantities of wool were shipped from the East Midlands to Lincoln's Waterside, seat of the wool staple, and thence to Flanders.

Over succeeding centuries the Fossdyke suffered from silting,

A view of Torksey Lock.

blockages and neglect. There was a mid-eighteenth century revival when the Ellison family financed improvements by charging tolls and dues. By the middle of the nineteenth century the arrival of the railways had caused widespread decline to canal traffic, but some carrying trade continued: Lincolnshire farm produce went to Torksey, as well as small quantities of coal, chemicals, timber and cottonseed brought in from the Midlands and the Humber. During the 1930's the barges of the Lincoln and Hull Water Transport Ltd. plied a steady trade, but by 1971 all commercial activity had ended, leaving the Fossdyke for water sports, social outings and fishermen.

Thus, Torksey developed as a vital junction for inland cargoes, and a focal point on England's oldest canal. Today the Lock presents a beautifully maintained scene of leisure boating with the week-end atmosphere of a marina.

Places of Interest in the Neighbourhood
47. That Village Sign (Saxilby)

The restored dovecote at Belleau.

49 A Manorial Dovecote

Position: Belleau is a hamlet about seven miles south-east of Louth
O.S. Map: Skegness, Sheet No. 122
Map Ref: TF 403/786
Access: Below the church a farm track, right, leads to the dovecote.

Although dovecotes were typical features of many medieval manors and monasteries, the right to keep pigeons was not extended to commoners until 1613. Pigeons provided a regular supply of eggs and they were useful for food, especially during the winter when meat supplies were uncertain.

Dovecotes fell into disuse as higher crop yields gradually enabled more animals to be kept through the winter. Several have survived in Lincolnshire eg. at Gunby Hall, near Spilsby (TF 465/668) and at Tattershall Castle (TF 212/576). This one at Belleau is unexpectedly large and was probably built during the sixteenth century. Octagonal in shape, it once had small openings on alternate sides but some have been blocked off. Considerable restoration took place in 1970, so it is a well-maintained and attractive survivor. It forms part of the estate of Belleau Manor.

Places of Interest in the Neighbourhood
50. A Versatile Buttercross (Burwell)

50 A Versatile Buttercross

Position: Burwell, six miles south of Louth
O.S. Map: Skegness, Sheet No. 121
Map Ref: TF 356/795
Access: By the A16.

There was a small market town at Burwell in the thirteenth century, and the Buttercross was built in the late seventeenth or early eighteenth century. Around it farm wives displayed their butter, cheese, eggs and poultry. Brick-built and octagonal, with a blank arch on each face, it seems to have been designed as a hall. The conical roof with an open cupola is a twentieth century addition. Since 1958 it has been used as a village hall.

Places of Interest in the Neighbourhood
49. A Manorial Dovecote (Belleau)
51. The Toll House Near the By-Pass (Louth)
52. A Famous Flood (Louth)

The old Buttercross at Burwell.

51 The Toll House Near the By-Pass

Position: Louth
O.S. Map: Skegness, Sheet No. 122
Map Ref: TF 319/860
Access: Hallington toll house is about a hundred yards north of the
A153 Horncastle Road and the A16 Boston-Grimsby Road.

The Hallington toll house is a particularly attractive survival and was
built in about 1770 when the Louth-Horncastle road was turnpiked.
Of brick and slate, it has original windows and a door on an angular
corner, with recesses on either side to fit toll charges. It is ironical that
the modern and very busy Louth by-pass is so near!

By 1837, the year of Queen Victoria's accession, Lincolnshire's
twenty-nine turnpike trusts, looking after some five hundred miles of
roads, were in decline. From the 1840's there was increasing competition from the railways, and only a few toll houses survive, as at
Sutterton (the round house, TF 286/352); and the greatly modified
sandstone Newstead Gatehouse (TF 047/078) on the Uffington Road
by the Stamford Cricket Ground. This old toll house still has the
original collector's box let into the wainscotting inside the door.

Places of Interest in the Neighbourhood
52. A Famous Flood (Louth)
58. Two Churches in One Yard (Alvingham)
60. A Mysterious White Lady (North Ormsby)

The Hallington toll-house, Louth.

52 A Famous Flood

Position: Louth
O.S. Map: Grimsby and Cleethorpes, Sheet No. 113
Map Ref: TF 326/875
Access: Bridge Street.

Bridge Street in Louth does not look particularly prone to flood waters. But appearances are sometimes deceptive, and Lincolnshire has an unenviable history of flood disasters – that immortalised in Jean Ingelow's poem of the 1571 floods, "High Tide on the Coast of Lincolnshire" – or those that devastated the Mablethorpe.district in 1953. But here is an account of the events that submerged inland Louth on Saturday, 29th May, 1920.

By early afternoon the sky was dark, and torrential rain began falling. The River Lud, swollen rapidly by waters pouring off the Wolds, overflowed and swept through the lower town. Within half an hour the level had risen fifteen feet. At the corner of James Street and Ramsgate Street three houses suffered structural damage. In Ermine Street floodwaters disabled the fire station. A garage was washed away. One lady stood by helplessly while her house and chickens were carried off. At one house Dr. Higgins rescued a drowning husband, delivered a baby and at length returned to find that his own home had been ruined.

By early evening two hundred houses were uninhabitable or destroyed; over a thousand people were homeless; and twenty-three were dead. Public buildings were requisitioned for accommodation, and army huts were erected on High Holme Road. A relief fund opened by the Mayor of Louth raised £90,000 to help the worst-stricken families.

In the London Road cemetery on the southern edge of the town, a memorial obelisk records the names and ages of the dead. They range from a little girl of one to an old man of eighty-two.

At the bridge on Bridge Street, a plaque has been let into the former mill-house wall to show the level reached by the flood waters. As you stand there today, looking some fifteen feet down at the quiet waters of the Lud, and back to the plaque, it is all difficult to believe.

Places of Interest in the Neighbourhood
51. The Toll House Near the By-Pass (Louth)
58. Two Churches in One Yard (Alvingham)
60. A Mysterious White Lady (North Ormsby)

The normally quiet waters of the River Lud at Bridge Street, Louth.

53 A Medieval Packhorse Bridge

Position: West Rasen
O.S. Map: Lincoln, Sheet No. 121
Map Ref: TF 064/893
Access: The bridge stands over the River Rase, and is situated between the post office and the church.

Curving over three ribbed arches, the cobbled surface of this old packhorse bridge provided just enough room for horse and rider. Packhorse conveyance had the advantage of allowing a few men to look after a large number of beasts travelling in single file. For collective security they might form a caravan, the front beast sometimes carrying a bell to warn other travellers.

Under a Tudor statute of 1555 parishes were responsible for their own roads, but there were many evasions. In rural areas, where ancient trade routes and ridgeway paths were used, improvements were delayed until the later years of the eighteenth century. This particular bridge has done well to survive, and combines with an attractive church and a thatched post office to make a delightful picture.

Other packhorse bridges are to be found at Scredington (TF 094/408) and Utterby (TF 305/933).

Places of Interest in the Neighbourhood
62. Brandy Wharf and Scrumpy (Brandy Wharf)

The ancient packhorse bridge at West Rasen.

54 A Maiden's Crown

Position: Springthorpe, four miles east of Gainsborough
O.S. Map: Lincoln, Sheet No. 121
Map Ref: SK 875/897
Access: St. Lawrence and St. George's Church.

On Shrove Tuesday 1814 a young lady called Mary Hill was ringing a church bell when her arm became entangled in the rope. She was carried up to the ceiling, banging her head before crashing to the floor. She died from her injuries. At her funeral, three maids in white, each carrying a white paper crown and white gloves, preceded the coffin. Afterwards the crowns were hung up inside the church. One is still there, preserved in a glass case by the font. A more recent replica hangs by the organ.

This sad souvenir belongs to a ritual that preceded the Reformation. William Shakespeare used "virgin rites" and "maiden strewments" at the funeral of Ophelia in *Hamlet*. Similar funeral customs were common in other parts of the country. Gloves and handkerchiefs were sometimes retained as tokens of remembrance in Derbyshire and parts of Yorkshire. It was once thought unlucky to move them. In practice they stay until they fall apart.

Places of Interest in the Neighbourhood
55. Hall and Kitchen Fit For a King (Gainsborough)
56. A May-Day Maypole (Hemswell)

55 Hall and Kitchen Fit For a King

Position: Gainsborough
O.S. Map: Scunthorpe, Sheet No. 112
Map Ref: SK 813/901
Access: The Old Hall stands at the junction of Gladstone Street and Parnell Street, between the parish church and the market place.

A first surprise is to find such an enormous brick and timber-framed manor house so near to the town centre. It was built between 1460 and 1480 for Sir Thomas Burgh, a locally powerful lord of the manor whose home had been destroyed during the War of the Roses. An early visitor (1483) was King Richard III. Henry VIII came in 1509, later meeting his last wife, Catherine Parr, in the town.

The Great Hall, with its spectacular braced wooden roof and magnificent beams, has also served also for religious meetings, as a linen factory, theatre, ballroom and auction room. Immediately off the Hall is a superb medieval kitchen, with two massive fireplaces, brick ovens and spits. In the north-east corner is a brick tower leading to bedrooms and ante-chambers, all tastefully furnished in period style.

Gainsborough Old Hall is rich in atmosphere, as well as a beautiful part of our heritage. It is open to visitors virtually all the year round.

Places of Interest in the Neighbourhood
54. A Maiden's Crown (Springthorpe)
56. A May-Day Maypole (Hemswell)

Gainsborough Old Hall: a delightful courtyard.

56 A May-Day Maypole

Position: Hemswell, just off the B1398, seven miles east of
Gainsborough
O.S. Map: Scunthorpe, Sheet No. 112
Map Ref: SK 929/909
Access: The maypole stands at the junction of Maypole Street and
Church Street.

The idea of dancing around a tree to celebrate the start of summer has
been traced to the ancient Celts. In medieval times maypole dancing
took place in many towns and villages so that maypoles became permanent fixtures on the green.

At Hemswell the tradition goes back at least to mid-Victorian times,

A street maypole at Hemswell.

for a newspaper tells of repairs in 1880. Older folk can remember taking part as children, cavorting around a small decorated pole in the school yard, in between enjoying refreshments at the fair. The custom lapsed for some years, but was renewed in time for the Royal Jubilee of 1977.

The life of a pole is surprisingly short. A number of old ones have been chopped up either for firewood or for such decorative purposes as door-stops. The present pole, rising some fifty feet, with red, white and blue spirals, dates from 1992, and is capped by a fox and weathervane. May Day revels draw large crowds to watch beribboned youngsters in Victorian costume turn and turn about, attended by Morris Men and Lincoln's Town Crier. It is said that refreshments are ample. May-Day in Hemswell is lavishly celebrated.

Places of Interest in the Neighbourhood
54. A Maiden's Crown (Springthorpe)
55. Hall and Kitchen Fit for a King (Gainsborough)

57 Our Smallest Post Office?

Position: Tealby
O.S. Map: Grimsby and Cleethorpes, Sheet No. 113
Map Ref: TF 156/904
Access: The Smooting, Front Lane.

Tealby is a charming Wolds village in an area of outstanding natural beauty. Many summer visitors in search of a postcard and a stamp may be surprised to find that the post office is part of the front room of a private house in a nineteenth century terrace. As the visitor enters, the others will have to form a queue outside, for inside there is little more than a square yard in which to conduct one's business. After business hours all signs of a post office are removed, and the premises revert to private use: the post box is a few yards away.

Running Tealby post office fairly close for size until its closure in 1992 was Thimbleby (TF 236/699), west of Horncastle, which consisted of a small weather-boarded pantiled shed.

Places of Interest in the Neighbourhood
53. A Medieval Packhorse Bridge (West Rasen)
61. Where Water Carts Queued (Binbrook)

58 Two Churches in One Yard

Position: Alvingham, three miles north-east of Louth
O.S. Map: Grimsby and Cleethorpes, Sheet No. 113
Map Ref: TF 367/914
Access: Church Lane, past the Water Mill (itself of considerable
interest) and straight through the farm yard – the accustomed route for
most parishioners. Or from North Cockerington, along the tow-path of
the Louth Navigation Canal and over the wooden bridge.

To find two churches, both twelfth century foundations, in one churchyard must be extremely unusual. Nearest the farm is St. Mary's of
North Cockerington, no longer used for regular worship, but remaining
a consecrated building maintained by the Redundant Churches Fund.
Its pews are still of the large box variety. In earlier centuries it may have
served as a chapel to the Gilbertine Priory which stood to the north of
the churchyard.

About twenty yards away is the parish church of Alvingham, St.
Adelwold's, believed to be the only church dedicated to this saint, who
was once a bishop on the island of Lindisfarne. The building was
considerably restored in 1933, and inside it is plain, inviting and well
cared for.

Places of Interest in the Neighbourhood
51. The Toll House Near the By-Pass (Louth)
52. A Famous Flood (Louth)
60. A Mysterious White Lady (North Ormsby)

St. Mary's Church, North Cockerington (left) alongside St. Adelwold's, Alvingham (right).

59 An Owlers' Haunt

Position: Saltfleet
O.S. Map: Grimsby and Cleethorpes, Sheet No. 113
Map Ref: TF 454/938
Access: The New Inn stands prominently by the main road on the seaward side.

Saltfleet is set in marshland, well back from the Haven, which was a minor port from Roman times until the eighteenth century. Coal and chalk were shipped in, and grain and salt shipped out. But this hinterland has enjoyed also many unofficial connections with sea traffic. Stories have been told of moving night lights, the clatter of hooves in the small hours, of lures and diversions aimed at Customs and Revenue men. After the prohibition of wool exports in 1672, much local wool was smuggled out of Saltfleet by night-operating 'Owlers'. Spirits, tobacco and silks, normally attracting heavy customs duties, were

Saltfleet's New Inn: a hostelry of legend.

smuggled in. Not without reason did gin become known as 'hollands'.

Despite its name (it was once called The Dolphin) the roomy New Inn is clearly an old building, dating from the seventeenth century or earlier. There used to be extensive stabling at the rear, and the gables and chimney stacks are enormous. To the right of the courtyard stands an old stone trough and a hand pump. Inside, the visitor is soon aware of flagstones, beams and unusual space. These rooms have provided shelter and refuge to generations of sailors, merchants and travellers, as well as many a smuggler eager for gossip of the local 'Revenue', for if caught and convicted an 'owler' could expect the lash, the noose or Botany Bay. Whether the legendary tunnel connecting the Inn and the nearby Tudor Manor actually existed must be a matter for speculation.

Places of Interest in the Neighbourhood
58. Two Churches in One Yard (Alvingham)

60 A Mysterious White Lady

Position: North Ormsby, five miles north-west of Louth
O.S. Map: Grimsby and Cleethorpes, Sheet No. 113
Map Ref: TF 278/929
Access: Field by Abbey Farm.

This Venusian life-size statue, of uncertain age, stands half-way up the hillside, amidst a line of trees and sheep walks. A local theory that she is of Roman antiquity is just possible, but her survival through war, invasion and vandalism must be considered remarkable.

Another suggestion is that she somehow derives from the Gilbertine Priory for nuns that developed this site seven centuries ago. But this is a worldly statue, lightly costumed, hardly a credible icon for a religious community dedicated to the Blessed Virgin. Or perhaps the statue may be in memory of a huntress thrown from her horse and killed in the locality. No-one knows. The White Lady remains an odd, haunting image presiding enigmatically over this edge of the Wolds.

Places of Interest in the Neighbourhood
51. The Toll House Near the By-Pass (Louth)
52. A Famous Flood (Louth)
58. Two Churches in One Yard (Alvingham)

North Ormsby's intriguing White Lady.

61 Where Water Carts Queued

Position: Binbrook
O.S. Map: Grimsby and Cleethorpes, Sheet No. 113
Map Ref: TF 213/943
Access: The pump is situated at the lower end of the Grimsby Road, at
the edge of the village.

During the nineteenth century many village pumps augmented the
supply from wells. They were generally of cast iron, some plain and
prosaic, others aesthetically pleasing, even picturesque. This Grimsby
Road pump was built on a ramp to enable water carts to fill up more
conveniently. Still embedded in the brickwork are three rings to which
waiting horses could be tethered. Hill farmers came down regularly into
the village to collect water needed at harvest time for steam-threshing
machines, as well as for brewing to quench the thirst of their workers.
The police station and magistrates' court, immediately opposite, would
doubtless guarantee a fairly orderly queue!

Many attractive pumps remain as curiosities in this county. The stone
'pepper pots' on Coleby village green are a particular delight (SK
975/606).

Places of Interest in the Neighbourhood
57. Our Smallest Post Office? (Tealby)
60. A Mysterious White Lady (North Ormsby)

A pump on a ramp at Binbrook.

62 Brandy Wharf and Scrumpy

Position: Brandy Wharf is about seven miles south-west of Caistor
O.S. Map: Scunthorpe, Sheet No. 112
Map Ref: TF 015/970
Access: Via the B1205 between Caistor and the A15 (Lincoln-Brigg).

This somewhat remote hamlet encapsulates much historical curiosity.
"Brande" may have been a Viking settler who used the River Ancholme
to and from Brigg. In medieval times there were several monasteries
close by, attracted, perhaps, by the river. When this new River
Ancholme was dug in the late eighteenth century to drain the area and
to replace the meandering old river for commercial purposes, Brandy
Wharf became a convenient depot. "The Anchor" was originally built
to accommodate navvies and watermen. Horse-drawn barges carried
cargoes of coal, timber, iron, lead, sand, slate and corn to and from
South Ferriby and the Humber.

Nowadays, apart from a warehouse and a few houses, the main focus
of interest is the pub. The Anchor is unusual in that it specialises in
cider. There is a choice of over fifty, many on draught, with a profusion
of pots, posters and mugs decorating the bar areas. Outside, a small
museum is crammed with some five hundred mugs, jugs and bottles
from all over Europe. An old apple orchard has been revived. The
barges have all gone, replaced by a shifting scene of dinghies and small
cruisers.

Places of Interest in the Neighbourhood
53. A Medieval Packhorse Bridge (West Rasen)
63. Pargeters' Place (Holton le Moor)

Brandy Wharf and the River Ancholme.

63 Pargeters' Place

Position: Holton le Moor, four miles south-west of Caistor
O.S. Map: Scunthorpe, Sheet No. 112
Map Ref: TF 082/977
Access: The Moot Hall is on the east side of the B1434 in the middle of the village.

Pargeting is a special art form which creates ornamental relief work on plastering or stucco. The brick buttressed, timber-framed Moot Hall built in 1910 provides many wonderful examples, especially of local and national historical themes. On the front of the building, to the left of the entrance, are panels illustrating birds, animals, fish, an anchor, shields, and an embossed 'Harmony' motif showing various musical instruments. There are also three village characters, including a shepherd. To the right are Nelson and Napoleon, whilst at the side are St. George and the Dragon, and St. Hugh alongside Lincoln Cathedral.

On a corner panel, Thomas George Dixon and his wife, Ethel Harriet

The pargeter's art: St. George killing the dragon, Holton le Moor.

have dedicated the Hall to the village as a public token of their twentieth wedding anniversary, making the pargeting a permanent record of celebration and thanksgiving. Immediately behind the Moot Hall is the village school, built in 1913. Above the front door is more pargetry, this time in colour. Spaced amidst floral branches and three shields are the words, "Live for God King Country".

Places of Interest in the Neighbourhood
62. Brandy Wharf and Scrumpy (Brandy Wharf)
67. The Caistor Gad Whip (Caistor)

Pargeting around the doorway of the Moot Hall, Holton le Moor.

64 The Haxey Hood

Position: Haxey
O.S. Map: Scunthorpe, Sheet No. 112
Map Ref: SK 764/998
Access: As several local hostelries compete annually for possession of
the Hood, visitors will need to inquire which inn currently holds it.

This seven hundred year old tradition started when Lady de Mowbray
lost her scarlet hood in a gale while on her way to a Twelfth Night
church service. Thirteen labourers dashed from their field to retrieve it,
resorting almost to fisticuffs for the privilege. So impressed was she by
this show of chivalry that she left thirteen acres of land to provide
money for the hood to be fought for annually by twelve men dressed in
scarlet jackets and velvet caps.

At 2.00 pm. on 6th January the bells of St. Nicholas Church announce
that the mêlée is imminent. The Fool, with dirty face, feathered hat, red
jumper, patched trousers and stringed bladder on a stick, is dragged
forward to a mounting block in front of the Church. As he re-tells the
origins of the occasion, damp straw is set alight near him and he leaps
to safety. The Lord of the Hood, clad in hunting coat and top hat
decorated with artificial flowers, and bearing his staff of thirteen willow
switches, deploys his chosen Boggins, each wearing a red jumper. A
number of canvas hoods are thrown up for a children's preliminary
scramble. Then the Lord, or a local celebrity, throws up the 'Hood' – a
two foot roll of tight sacking – and the game begins. Scores of young
men form a 'sway' (local word) for possession of the hood, trying to
drag it to their favourite pub. This huge sweating scrum often continues
its struggle well into the evening. Finally, the hood is deemed to have
crossed into the precincts of a Haxey pub. The red-ribboned ceremonial
leather Hood is hung triumphantly in the bar, and there are free drinks
for the winners. The rest of the evening is devoted to toasting the suc-
cess of another Hood, and the Hood Dance at the Memorial Hall.

Places of Interest in the Neighbourhood
68. He Preached on His Father's Tomb (Epworth)

65 A Deserted Medieval Village and Thieves' Stronghold

Position: Gainsthorpe is 1³/₄ miles south of Hibaldstow
O.S. Map: Scunthorpe, Sheet No. 112
Map Ref: SE 955/013
Access: The Gainsthorpe Road should be taken on the west side of the
A15. After about 400 yards a farm road, left, leads to the site.

Gainsthorpe immediately shows the mounds and depressions associated with deserted medieval villages, even the tentative identification of roads and 'platforms' as likely sites for buildings. There are a
considerable number of rectangular plots, indicating, perhaps, former
yards, paddocks and gardens. The impression grows that here was once
a planned, well-established community of some size, for the findings
include Roman coins, pottery, bricks and the remains of a tessellated
pavement. The village was, of course, very close to Ermine Street. It

An aerial view of the deserted medieval village of Gainsthorpe.

was mentioned in the Domesday Survey (1086) and the last written record was from 1383.

Whether or not it owed its decline to the Black Death, more than a generation earlier, it was certainly used later by highwaymen as a shelter and handy base for intercepting travellers en route to and from Lincoln. In 1697 the village was visited by Abraham de la Pryme, famous diarist and curate of Broughton, who noted the vestiges of over a hundred houses and described the impact of the highwaymen: "Their great robberies were one of the causes that made this road (Ermine Street) to be neglected and travellers durst not pass but in caravans together." Another story tells of a determined local uprising which not only cleared Gainsthorpe of its criminal fraternity, but afterwards burnt the village so as to discourage their return.

Lincolnshire has a considerable number of other deserted village sites, three of the most interesting being at Riseholme, to the north of Lincoln (SK 985/754); Brauncewell, five miles north-west of Sleaford (TF 046/525); and Stallingborough, four miles north-west of Grimsby (TA 195/116).

Places of Interest in the Neighbourhood
62. Brandy Wharf and Scrumpy (Brandy Wharf)
66. A Derelict Lime Kiln (Kirton in Lindsey)
74. Brigg Fair (Brigg)

The Kirton Lime Kiln.

66 A Derelict Lime Kiln

Position: 1 ½ miles north-east of Kirton-in-Lindsey
O.S. Map: Scunthorpe, Sheet No. 112
Map Ref: SE 948/013
Access: Up the Gainsthorpe Road off the west side of the A15. Look for old Blue Cement works, left, after half a mile. The kiln is visible to the right. It can be reached by taking the track to the left of the Kirton Lime Sidings signal box.

During medieval times many English villages developed their own lime kilns, and burning lime for agricultural purposes has been known in the Hibaldstow/Kirton-in-Lindsey area since at least the 1820's. This impressive kiln, now a Grade II listed building, was constructed in the later nineteenth century as part of the Blue Lias Lime and Cement Works. The tapering tower was itself built of squared limestone, lined with bricks, and shows a number of brick-arched openings and tunnel vaults. During the burning process limestone and coal were layered in the ratio of 4 to 1, and carbon dioxide was given off to leave quick lime.

Alongside are the Kirton Lime Sidings, formerly linked to the Great Central Line, which brought West Riding coal via Gainsborough and provided a distribution network for the products of lime and cement.

As a modernised cement industry developed on the adjacent site, the kiln was eventually abandoned. Now both have run their course and the works are deserted.

Places of Interest in the Neighbourhood
62. Brandy Wharf and Scrumpy (Brandy Wharf)
65. A Deserted Medieval Village and Thieves' Stronghold (Gainsthorpe)
74. Brigg Fair (Brigg)

67 The Caistor Gad Whip

Position: Caistor
O.S. Map: Grimsby and Cleethorpes, Sheet No. 113
Map Ref: TA 117/013
Access: The Church of St. Peter and St. Paul is below the market place.

Caistor was once the home of a unique Palm Sunday ritual that involved the tenants of nearby Broughton providing a ploughman's whip (or goad) to be taken to Caistor Church. Attached securely to the top of the stock was a purse containing thirty coins. During the first lesson of Matins, the designated tenant would crack the whip three times in the north porch before taking it inside. During the second lesson he cracked the whip thrice over the minister's head, then held it still until the lesson was concluded. The whip, with lash folded round the seven foot stock, was then ceremonially placed in the pew of the Lord of Hundon Manor.

While this ceremony was obviously rich in symbolism, its precise significance is not clear. One theory likens the three whip cracks to Peter's denials of Jesus, while the thirty coins obviously represent Judas Iscariot's blood money. A homelier legend attributes the origins to a self-imposed punishment by the Squire of Hundon for having dealt too severely with a young trespasser.

It is conceivable that the Gad Whip ceremony started in Reformation times. But during the nineteenth century it attracted considerable adverse publicity and noisy behaviour and sadly fell victim to the Victorian belief that such rituals were out of place in a church. The ceremony was last performed in 1846 when Hundon Manor changed hands. The relic is mounted in a glass case on the north wall of the church.

Places of Interest in the Neighbourhood
63. Pargeters' Place (Holton le Moor)
73. Beauty in Stone and Marble (Great Limber)

68 He Preached on His Father's Tomb

Position: Epworth
O.S. Map: Scunthorpe, Sheet No. 112
Map Ref: SE 782/038
Access: From the market place Church Street leads to St. Andrew's
Church. The tomb is immediately seen to the right of the south door.

John Wesley was born at Epworth in 1703, the fifteenth of nineteen
children. The life of this greatest of all English preachers was packed
with incident, and before he was six he had been snatched from his
home when a group of parishioners set fire to it. As the son of an
impoverished clergymen he was obliged to live frugally at Oxford, once
walking the entire hundred and fifty miles home.

Wesley's turning point took place in May 1738, when he underwent a
renewed spiritual conversion at an Assembly in Aldersgate. He became

The Wesley Tomb in Epworth Churchyard.

an inspired and indomitable preacher, attracting enormous crowds in London and Bristol. When churches could not accommodate his congregations he turned to open-air addresses. Back in Epworth in June 1742 he was refused permission to speak in the church. So he mounted his father's tomb and was received rapturously. It was the start of a lifetime's work.

His reception varied. On his home ground he was popular. He often spoke from the market cross in Epworth Square, as the plaque testifies. Brigg he found "a noisy turbulent town". At Gainsborough in 1759 he was met by "a rude, wild multitude". At Horncastle, too, was "a wild, unbroken herd". Despite these set-backs John Wesley travelled a quarter of a million miles on horseback, preached some forty thousand sermons and somehow managed to write over two hundred books. Epworth's greatest son, Wesley is remembered world-wide as the founder of the Methodist Church.

Epworth is a place of pilgrimage. The delightful Old Rectory, built in Queen Anne style, contains many memorabilia. The market cross is popular with photographers, and the tomb of the Rev. Samuel and Susannah Wesley is a place for peace and reflection.

A well-known painting of the tomb-preaching incident by George Wadington Brownlow (1835-76) may be seen in the Banqueting Hall of the Guildhall, Boston (TF 337/432).

Places of Interest in the Neighbourhood
64. The Haxey Hood (Haxey)

69 Where East Meets West

Position: Cleethorpes
O.S. Map: Grimsby and Cleethorpes, Sheet No. 113
Map Ref: TA 327/067
Access: On the south side of the town follow the Marine Embankment
as far as the Golf Course. The signpost stands out clearly on the Shore
footpath, which is crossed by the Greenwich Meridian Line.

According to Rudyard Kipling, east was east and west was west, and
never the twain should meet. Yet at the Meridian they do. 'Meridian'
(from the Latin 'meridies') means midday. In 1884 the Greenwich
Meridian was established by international consent as the line from
which longitude and time should be calculated. Lincolnshire is unusual
in having three towns that bestride the Greenwich Prime Meridian of 0°
longitude.

At Cleethorpes a metal arrow set diagonally across the Shore footpath is inscribed "THIS IS THE LINE OF THE GREENWICH
MERIDIAN LONGITUDE 0° 0′ 0″". A signpost indicates that the
distance to the North Pole is 2,517 miles, to the South Pole 9,919, to
New York 3,418, to London 143 and to Moscow 1,495 miles. It is
tempting to pose for a photograph with one foot in the western and the
other in the eastern hemisphere.

At Louth on a wall at 105 Eastgate Street (TF 332/875) the meridian
is marked by a plaque showing an aeroplane flying over a sailing ship.
At Wignals Gate, on the western side of Holbeach (TF 354/248) 0°
Longitude is indicated by a millstone set up in 1959 by the East Elloe
Rural District Council.

Places of Interest in the Neighbourhood
70. Grim and Havelock (Grimsby)
71. The National Fishing Heritage Centre (Grimsby)
72. Italianate and Tallest (Grimsby)

70 Grim and Havelock

Position: Grimsby
O.S. Map: Grimsby and Cleethorpes, Sheet No. 113
Map Ref: TS 266/079
Access: Approached via the A46 Grimsby-Caistor Road is the Grimsby College of Technology and Arts. The statue stands in the College grounds, readily seen from the Fryston Corner roundabout.

This statue showing Grim bearing the young Havelock on his shoulders recalls the Viking saga of the origins of Grimsby. When Grim, a poor fisherman, found a drifting boat containing the young Havelock, he adopted the princely outcast as one of his own. Havelock eventually became a kitchen scullion in the Lincoln home of the treacherous Earl Goderich, who, coveting the fortune of his ward, Goldborough, married her off to Havelock. Goldborough and Havelock soon came to realise that they had been cheated of their respective inheritances. Accordingly, Havelock, supported by Grim and a huge army, sailed to Denmark to regain the usurped crown. On their return to England Havelock's followers easily routed Goderich. The faithful and gallant Grim was now richly rewarded; and their village was renamed Grimsby.

Interesting as the legend is, its reliability is open to doubt. Yet a twelfth century Borough Seal shows Grim with sword and shield, Goldborough to one side and Havelock, with crown, on the other. The tale has been commemorated more recently by this superbly sculpted bronze statue of Grim and Havelock by local artist, Wayne Hobson, unveiled in 1973.

Places of Interest in the Neighbourhood
69. Where East Meets West (Cleethorpes)
71. The National Fishing Heritage Centre (Grimsby)
72. Italianate and Tallest (Grimsby)

Grim shouldering the little outcast, Havelock. The statue stands in front of Grimsby's College of Technology and Arts.

71 The National Fishing Heritage Centre

Position: Grimsby
O.S. Map: Grimsby and Cleethorpes, Sheet No. 113
Map Ref: TA 269/098
Access: From the M180 go to Victoria Street North. The Centre, which is well sign-posted, is behind the Alexandra Dock.

The National Fishing Heritage Centre, opened in 1990, re-creates convincingly the living and working conditions on a trawler of the 1950's. Experiences are offered of the cramped living quarters, the pitch and roll of the vessel, the heat of the engine room, and the sub-freezing cold of an Arctic night. All the scenarios are imaginatively enhanced by carefully simulated sound and colour effects. Visitors are likely to emerge with a heightened respect for an earlier generation of Grimsby trawlermen, and they will understand why this Centre quickly became an award-winning museum.

Outside again, in the calmer waters of the dock, is the Boston shrimper, *Perseverance.* In the nearby Alexandra Dock the former Grimsby trawler, the *Ross Tiger,* may be visited. Moored there, too, is the restored 600 ton paddle-steamer, *Lincoln Castle,* which once ferried passengers from Hull to New Holland in the days before the Humber Bridge, and is now a popular restaurant and conference centre.

Places of Interest in the Neighbourhood
69. Where East Meets West (Cleethorpes)
70. Grim and Havelock (Grimsby)
72. Italianate and Tallest (Grimsby)

72 Italianate and Tallest

Position: Grimsby north, dock area.
O.S. Map: Grimsby and Cleethorpes, Sheet No. 113
Map Ref: TA 278/113
Access: East Side Royal Dock and Fish Dock Road, then follow the
road to the Tidal Basin by the Humber and so to the base of the Tower.

Standing 313 feet high, this redbrick tower is the county's tallest building, exceeding Louth Parish Church (295 ft.), Boston Stump (272 ft.) and Lincoln Cathedral (271 feet). Its walls are four feet thick at the base, and approximately one million bricks were used in its construction. Designed by J. W. Wild after the campanile of the Palazzo Pubblico of Siena, it was completed in 1851. Near the top each wall face

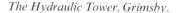

The Hydraulic Tower, Grimsby.

turns outward to support a line of five arches, and just below the surmounting lantern is another arcade of four. Three window slits repeated geometrically at six levels have been filled in to keep out pigeons.

Constructed on a pier between two lock-pits, the Hydraulic Tower's functions were to activate ten pairs of lock gates, crossing gates and cranes on the Royal Dock. Its high tank held 26,500 gallons of water, pumped from a well by two steam engines. Forty years later the work was taken over by the nearby smaller tower (78 feet) which provided a high pressure hydraulic system until it, too, was made redundant by a modern oil-hydraulic operation.

For Grimbarians, the tower is as dominant as the Eiffel Tower is to Parisians, symbolising the great days when the town was the world's largest fishing port. A listed building which even appears on the mayoral chain of office, it is the property of Associated British Ports.

Places of Interest in the Neighbourhood
69. Where East Meets West (Cleethorpes)
70. Grim and Havelock (Grimsby)
71. The National Fishing Heritage Centre (Grimsby)

73 Beauty in Stone and Marble

Position: Great Limber, eight miles west of Grimsby
O.S. Map: Grimsby and Cleethorpes, Sheet No. 113
Map Ref: TA 134/089
Access: On the north side of the A18 about 150 yards east of the small
square is a lay-by from which it is but a short walk through the wood to
the Mausoleum. Visitors wishing to enter the building must arrange
with the keyholder who lives at the house in the square that displays the
black Yarborough 'Buckle' crest. A visitors' book may be signed.

Situated on an ancient burial mound in attractive parkland at the edge
of the Brocklesby Estate is this supremely satisfying mausoleum, completed in 1792 by James Wyatt. It was built by the first Lord Yarborough as a memorial to his young wife, Sophia Aufrere who died in

Brocklesby Mausoleum.

Inside the Mausoleum at Brocklesby: the marble statue of Sophia Aufrere.

1787. The circular temple with twelve fluted Doric columns and a flattened glass dome is based on the Temples of Vesta at Tivoli and Rome. Inside, beneath a dome full of angels, the focus is a marble statue of Sophia by Joseph Nollekens.

On another part of the estate, one mile north-east of Caistor (TA 129/031) is Pelham's Pillar, 128 feet tall and visible for miles. It was started in 1840 to commemorate the planting of some twelve and a half million trees between 1787 and 1828 by the same Charles Anderson Pelham, first Lord Yarborough.

Places of Interest in the Neighbourhood
78. A Wayside Gallows (Melton Ross)
79. The Pilgrim Fathers' Memorial (Immingham)

74 Brigg Fair

Position: Brigg
O.S. Map: Scunthorpe, Sheet No. 112
Map Ref: TA 004/073
Access: Market Place.

Restored toll boards are curiosities indeed. Those mounted in Brigg Market Place and in adjacent streets are reminders of the variety of animals that were brought to the famous Fair, and of the charges made. The Fair derived from a charter granted by Henry III in 1236, and by 1752 it took place annually on August 5th. It stretched across the Market Place from the Buttercross, past the Angel Hotel and down

A toll board for Brigg Fair.

BRIGG URBAN DISTRICT COUNCIL
TABLE OF TOLLS

For every Head of Cattle	2ᴅ
For every Calf	1ᴅ
For every Sheep or Lamb	1ᴅ
For every Pig	2ᴅ
For every Horse	6ᴅ
For every Cᵂᵀ of Potatoes	1ᴅ
For every Basket of Fruit	1ᴅ
For every Basket of Butter	2ᴅ
For every Basket of Eggs	2ᴅ
For every Couple of Fowl or Ducks	1ᴅ
For every Goose	1ᴅ
For every Turkey	2ᴅ
For every Couple of Rabbits	1ᴅ
For every Half Dozen Pigeons	1ᴅ

*As Approved by the Minister
of Health July 1921 C.F.W. Cotton
Clerk to the Council*

to the River Ancholme, offering boat-races, travelling theatre bands, dances and other amusements.

Early this century an old folk song, 'Brigg Fair', became a landmark in the history of recorded music when Percy Grainger, the Australian composer, was in Brigg collecting songs that were in danger of being lost. After being impressed by the voice of a local singer, Joseph Taylor, a gamekeeper at Saxby-all-Saints, Grainger sent his phonograph recording of 'Brigg Fair' to his friend, Frederick Delius, who immortalised the song as an orchestral rhapsody. Invited to London for its first performance, Taylor rose from the dress circle and sang the words again. It is thought that Grainger's subsequent collection of Lincolnshire folk songs was among the first to be mechanically recorded.

Places of Interest in the Neighbourhood
76. A Roman Mosaic Mural (Scunthorpe)
77. Tuffa the Hillside Dragon (Dragonby)
78. A Wayside Gallows (Melton Ross)

The last Teesside trolley bus.

75 Back to the 'Trackless'

Position: Sandtoft is 7 miles west of Scunthorpe
O.S. Map: Scunthorpe, Sheet No. 112
Map Ref: SE 746/082
Access: Sandtoft is just off the M180, near Junction 2. The Transport
Centre is at Belton Road, open on Sunday afternoons,
April-September, plus several days advertised every year.

Trolleybuses or 'Trackless' first operated in Leeds and Bradford in
1911, working on an electrical circuit using 550-600 volts D.C. During
their peak years in the later 1940's fifty British towns and cities were
using them. Motor-bus competition made them less competitive, and
their inexorable decline ended on 26th March 1972 when the last
trolleybus halted in Bradford.

In 1969 part of the former RAF Sandtoft was acquired by a group of
trolleybus enthusiasts. Gradually they have bought over sixty vehicles
to form the largest collection in the United Kingdom. The oldest is a
1927 Garrett bus from Mexborough and Swinton. The last Bradford
trolleybus is here. There are several from abroad, including one from
Aachen (1956) and Liege (1932). Within Lincolnshire, Cleethorpes had
fifteen trolleybuses as late as 1953 but none has survived.

On Trolley Days the buses are brought out of the depot and linked to
the overhead circuit so that visitors may enjoy a short and surprisingly
quiet ride.

Places of Interest in the Neighbourhood
68. He Preached on His Father's Tomb (Epworth)
76. A Roman Mosaic Mural (Scunthorpe)
77. Tuffa the Hillside Dragon (Dragonby)

76 A Roman Mosaic Mural

Position: Central Park Scunthorpe
O.S. Map: Scunthorpe, Sheet No. 112
Map Ref: SE 889/103
Access: Civic Centre, off Ashby Road.

Set amidst carefully tended gardens, the Civic Centre has this large Roman-British mosaic mounted as the focus of its entrance hall. The mosaic was excavated in 1959 from a Roman villa at Winterton, four miles to the north-east, and presented to Scunthorpe Borough Council by the Sawyer family. Other important archaeological finds have been made in the area, which is close to the Roman Ermine Street.

The centre panel shows Ceres, the Goddess of Agriculture, holding a torch. It is wholly appropriate, but still historically curious, that a mosaic with this theme should be re-discovered after nearly two millennia, in this the granary of England.

Places of Interest in the Neighbourhood
74. Brigg Fair (Brigg)
75. Back to the 'Trackless' (Sandtoft)
77. Tuffa the Hillside Dragon (Dragonby)

The Ceres Mosaic, Scunthorpe Civic Centre.

77 Tuffa the Hillside Dragon

Position: Dragonby, two miles north of Scunthorpe
O.S. Map: Scunthorpe, Sheet No. 112
Map Ref: SE 905/143
Access: Halfway down the village street the unpaved road ('tenfoot') on the right dwindles into a footpath. Fifty yards further on is the field with the dragon on the hillside.

Dragonby village derives its name from this curious 'dragon'. Geologically, the dragon is a tuffa, a limestone deposit left by an ancient spring which once ran down the hillside. It looks most realistic, as a dragon couchant should. From head to twisting tail it measures about thirty yards; there is a deep groove down its back and lifelike indentations behind the head.

Folk explanations have had ample time to ripen. One popular tale had it that the beast had plagued a flock of sheep, and that the shepherd finally lost patience and turned him to stone.

Places of Interest in the Neighbourhood
74. Brigg Fair (Brigg)
75. Back to the 'Trackless' (Sandtoft)
76. A Roman Mosaic Mural (Scunthorpe)

78 A Wayside Gallows

Position: Western edge of Melton Ross
O.S. Map: Scunthorpe Area, Sheet No. 112
Map Ref: TA 045/106
Access: Melton Ross is on the A18 Brigg to Grimsby Road. The Gallows is immediately behind the lay-by west of Gallows Hill filling station.

This curious gallows looks like a rural goalpost. It serves, however, as a reminder of a grimmer game that was played hereabouts between two local families in the early seventeenth century.

Melton was the seat of the Ross family; the Tyrwhitts lived at nearby Kettleby. Differences probably starting as social rivalry and taken up by servants and partisan supporters hardened into a feud. During a hunting expedition retainers of the two families met and came to blows, and men on both sides were killed. News of the skirmish reached James I, who was paying a visit to Lincolnshire. Horrified to learn that the royal peace could be so readily flouted, the King ordered a gallows to be built on the site. Any deaths arising from future Ross/Tyrwhitt encounters would be regarded as murder, and the perpetrators hanged.

Places of Interest in the Neighbourhood
73. Beauty in Stone and Marble (Great Limber)
74. Brigg Fair (Brigg)
80. Thornton Abbey (Thornton Curtis)

'Gallows' at Melton Ross.

79 The Pilgrim Fathers' Memorial

Position: St. Andrew's Green, Immingham
O.S. Map: Grimsby & Cleethorpes, Sheet No. 113.
Map Ref: TA 188/145
Access: From the main shopping thoroughfare, Washdyke Lane leads directly onto Church Lane. The Green is at the bottom, opposite St. Andrew's Church.

This fine monument, built by the Anglo-American Society to mark the tri-centenary of the Pilgrim Fathers' epic voyage, rests upon a plinth of grey granite brought from Plymouth Rock, Massachusetts, where the *Mayflower* landed in December 1620. For forty-five years it stood at Immingham Creek, but as access became difficult the monument was

The Pilgrim Fathers' Memorial

re-erected in this quiet open space in May 1970.

It was from the Creek in 1609 that a large number of Lincolnshire folk, together with friends from beyond the Trent, had left for Holland, en route to the New World "in search of religious liberty", as the memorial reminds us. Owing to many delays and tribulations, however, it was not until 1620 that they were able to set out on the final leg of their journey from Plymouth for New England.

Places of Interest in the Neighbourhood
70. Grim and Havelock (Grimsby)
71. The National Fishing Heritage Centre (Grimsby)
72. Italianate and Tallest (Grimsby)
73. Beauty in Stone and Marble (Great Limber)

Thornton Abbey: a magnificent gatehouse.

80 Thornton Abbey

Position: Three miles south-east of Barrow upon Humber
O.S. Map: Grimsby & Cleethorpes: Sheet No. 113
Map Ref: TA 114/189
Access: The gatehouse, dominant in this landscape, is well signposted
and lies just off the minor road between Thornton Curtis village and
East Halton.

The magnificent gate-house at Thornton Abbey, believed to be the
largest in England, was completed in 1382, and at first sight resembles
the front of a fortified manor. Four octagonal turrets and numerous
arrow slits certainly lend a defensive flavour, and close inspection of the
main arch confirms that there was once a portcullis. Above it is a statue
of the Virgin Mary, flanked by William le Gros, the Abbey's founder
and a crook-bearing abbot. While some of the canopied niches retain
the images of saints, many are now empty.

Behind this towering facade a winding staircase gives access to the
Great Hall on the first floor as well as other rooms and passages. From
the top, on a fine day, there are extensive views to the Humber.

Little survives of the rest of the Abbey, founded in 1139. Fragments of
stone outline the huge area of the former church. Vestiges of the south
transept remain, as does part of the octagonal chapter house. Excavations in 1722 revealed behind an adjacent wall a skeleton seated at a
table with a book and candlestick.

Soon after the Dissolution in 1539, Henry VIII came here with
Catherine Howard and held meetings of the Privy Council. The Abbey
was re-founded as a college of secular canons – an exceptional reprieve
which lasted only until the king's death in 1547. Several subsequent
owners, like the Earls of Yarborough, used the gatehouse as a dwelling.

The site is currently maintained by the Department of the Environ-
ment. Visitors are welcome from 10.00 a.m. to 6.00 p.m., April-September; and from 10.00 a.m. to 4.00 p.m. from October to March, apart
from the Christmas period.

Places of Interest in the Neighbourhood
78. A Wayside Gallows (Melton Ross)
79. The Pilgrim Fathers' Memorial (Immingham)
81. *'Amy Howson'* (South Ferriby)

81 'Amy Howson'

Position: South Ferriby Marina (summer)
O.S. Map: Scunthorpe Sheet No. 112
Map Ref: SE 975/210
Access: From the road by the Ferriby Sluice is a footpath leading to the Marina.

The Humber sloop, like its companion vessel, the keel, has a long ancestry reminiscent of Viking longships. Instead of the single square sail, however, the sloop's fore and main sails provide ready identification.

This lone survivor was built at Beverley in 1904 as a keel and christened *Sophia*. Her first work was carrying coal from Sheffield to Beverley. In 1916 she was re-rigged as a sloop for transporting goods between Hull and Grimsby, with a change of name to *I Know*. Six years later William Henry Barraclough of Barton on Humber acquired her and changed the name again, this time to that of his daughter, *Amy Howson*. For many years the sloop was engaged in carrying chemicals and oilseed about the Humber ports, but was finally moored up the River Hull, where her condition deteriorated.

In 1976 *Amy* was acquired by the Humber Keel and Sloop Preservation Society, and once again re-rigged as a sloop. The *Amy Howson* was the first vessel to sail under the Humber Bridge on its opening day, 17th July 1981. She now makes regular cruises on the Humber and River Ancholme, and is occasionally exhibited on the Trent, and at Brigg and Lincoln. During the winter months she retires to Barton Haven.

Places of Interest in the Neighbourhood
80. Thornton Abbey (Thornton Curtis)
82. Julian's Bower (Alkborough)

124

Amy Howson *in full sail.*

82 Julian's Bower

Position: Alkborough, seven miles north of Scunthorpe
O.S. Map: Scunthorpe, Sheet No. 112
Map Ref: SE 880/218
Access: At Countess Close off Back Street.

Very few turf mazes survive, but their beginnings owe much to classical themes. According to one account, Julius, son of Aeneas, the legendary founder of Rome, brought the idea of the maze from Troy to Italy; so turf mazes often became 'Julian's Bower'. Patterns starting from a central cross and representing the Christian quest for salvation were adopted by the early Church.

It is thought that this one, high above the Trent Falls, may have been cut some seven centuries ago by Benedictine monks from nearby Walcot Abbey. In the adjacent eleventh century Church of St. John the Baptist the maze design lies on a stone in the porch. Above the altar the top window shows yet another maze image.

Places of Interest in the Neighbourhood
76. A Roman Mosaic Mural (Scunthorpe)
77. Tuffa the Hillside Dragon (Dragonby)
81. *'Amy Howson'* (South Ferriby)

Alkborough: the medieval turf maze.

Index

The Curiosities of England

The following titles in the series have already been published and can be ordered at all bookshops, or in case of difficulties direct from the publishers.